all the best
CONTESTS
for kids

Two New Contests!

If you're under 13, we have two great contests for you.

Contest #1—Count the Fuzzdips

 If you saw the first two editions of **All the Best Contests for Kids,** you remember the little creatures hidden in them. First, they were called "Glitsches." Then Jennifer Helfand of Narberth, Pennsylvania, named them "Fuzzdips." They're still called Fuzzdips, and they're back! Count them and tell us how many there are. Everyone who enters will get a Fuzzdip Finder certificate. If you find them all, we'll send you a great surprise.

Contest #2—Design-a-Birthday-Card Contest

This is a chance for you to design a birthday card for a friend or family member. These are the rules for your card:

1. It should be on a piece of paper folded in half. When folded, the card must be 5½ by 7 inches.
2. The card must have art on the front and a written message inside. If you want to, you can put art inside also. The back should be blank.
3. You can use crayons, paint, markers, colored pencils, or any other flat medium.
4. All cards must be original. Your message and picture must be your own ideas.
5. One of your parents must sign the official entry form or a letter containing that information.
6. The judges will evaluate your card on originality, sincerity, and artistic merit. The way the art relates to the message is also important.

Winners will receive fantastic books and glow-in-the-dark posters from Ten Speed Press and exciting hobby kits from The Activities Club. Winning cards will also be published in the next edition of **All the Best Contests for Kids.**

Count the Fuzzdips

Name _____

Address _____

City _____ State _____ Zip _____

Phone (include area code) _____

Date of Birth _____

Number of Fuzzdips _____

Your parent's signature for consent to use your name in future editions of ALL THE BEST CONTESTS FOR KIDS and all associated promotional activities:

_____

Your entry must be postmarked by January 1, 1993 and sent to:

THE ACTIVITIES CLUB–FUZZDIPS
P.O. Box 9104
Waltham, MA 02254-9104

Design-a-Birthday Card

Name _____

Address _____

City _____ State _____ Zip _____

Phone (include area code) _____

Date of Birth _____

Your parent's signature below states that the work submitted is original and is done by you alone. It also gives us consent to use your art and your name in future editions of ALL THE BEST CONTESTS FOR KIDS and all associated promotional activities:

_____

Your entry must be postmarked by March 1, 1993 and sent to:

THE ACTIVITIES CLUB–CARD
P.O. Box 9104
Waltham, MA 02254-9104

all the best
CONTESTS
for kids
1992 • 1993

Joan M. Bergstrom and Craig Bergstrom

1○ Ten Speed Press
Berkeley, California

1◉ TEN SPEED PRESS
P.O. Box 7123
Berkeley, California 94707

Text design by Canterbury Press
Cover design by Fifth Street Design

Library of Congress Cataloging-in-Publication Data
Bergstrom, Joan M.
    All the best contests for kids, 1992–1993 / Joan Bergstrom & Craig Bergstrom.
        p.   cm.
    Summary: Provides information about various types of contests and how to decide which are the best to enter. Also includes ideas for sponsoring and running contests.
    ISBN 0-89815-451-0
    1. Contests—Juvenile literature. 2. Contests—United States—Directories—Juvenile literature. [1. Contests.] I. Bergstrom, Craig. II. Title.
GV1201.6.B474   1992
790.1'34—dc20   91-37659
                                                      CIP

Printed in the United States of America

1 2 3 4 5 — 96 95 94 93 92

Table of Contents

More Thanks!

This is our third edition of **All the Best Contests for Kids.** We are delighted to find that our book is still valued and appreciated.

We are especially grateful that the second edition of **All the Best Contests for Kids** was awarded the Parents' Choice Award in Doing and Learning.

We would like to thank all the kids who have written to us. Some enter our contests, some tell us about contests they've entered, and some let us know about new contests. We appreciate hearing from all of them.

When we first discussed the book with Phil and Winifred Wood, they thought it should be a regular publication. Those who know them will not be surprised to hear that they were right.

George Young and Mariah Bear worked hard to make the pile of papers that we sent them into a real book.

Finally, Gary was, just as in the first two editions, always a source of encouragement and support.

Dear Kids,

This book was written just for you. It was written for those of you who like to read about contests and other fun things to do. And it was written for those of you who actually like to take part in all kinds of contests. If you like to enter contests, then this book will tell you about many contests you might like to try or explain others that you had thought about entering, but were afraid to try. The contests in the book range all the way from pie eating and frog jumping to speed skating to photography, and just about everything in between. There are even our two contests for you right in this book. (All the information about our two contests and the entry forms for them are in the front of this book.)

Some of the contests in this book are held only in certain parts of the country, and you may live too far from them to be able to participate. We have included them because we thought they were interesting and unusual. You might consider taking one of them as a model for a similar contest in your neighborhood, club, school, or town. If you would like to do this, this book will give you lots of ideas about how to go setting up and running some exciting contests.

In addition to all the information on contests, we also tell you about over a hundred magazines, newspapers, and book publishers that print stories, poems, puzzles, drawings, etc., created by children. Some of them run contests of their own. Some of them might even pay you a small amount of money if they publish your material. If you like to write, you will find many opportunities to get your work published.

We hope you have fun "contesting," and wish you luck in our two contests and in any other you might enter or plan for your friends. And remember, if you don't try, you can't be a winner! Have fun!

Joan Bergstrom

Craig Bergstrom

Dear Parents and
After-School and Club Leaders,

All the Best Contests for Kids describes many contests and writing opportunities for children between the ages of 6 and 12. We wrote this book because we know that kids love creative and physical activities and that, with rare exceptions, they love contests, too. There's the intensity of competing, the agony of losing, occasionally the thrill of winning, and always the fun of participating.

Beyond good fun, though, we know that there are many other benefits to "contesting" that give this book a more serious purpose. Most of these benefits have to do with constructive use of that most precious commodity—a child's time. Few people realize that children between the ages of 6 and 12 spend nearly 80% of their waking time out of school. If you add up the hours before and after school, and weekends and vacations, it comes to 195 full days. Most children spend far too many of these hours in front of a television set because they have nothing else to do.

Not only do children in this 6-to-12 age group have a lot of "free" time to spend, but also this particular age span is a vital one in terms of child development. In middle childhood, children want to make things, do things, become good at something, and master what they do. It is during these years that children learn to read and write, and develop many specific skills, lifelong interests, and competencies. These are the interpretive years, rich with possibilities, and the time when critical foundations are laid for adolescence and beyond. It is essential that we adults guide our children toward activities that promote growth.

Psychoanalyst Erik Erikson explains that a healthy personality in children 6 to 12 years old is built on the development of a "sense of industry." Erikson's term, "industry," refers to the enormous interest children this age have in learning how things work, in constructing and building practical things, in creating many different kinds of items—all important elements of contests. Erikson feels that children's sense of industry is supported when their efforts are encouraged. If they are allowed to finish their work and are praised or rewarded for their efforts, their natural inclination to feel pride in their industry is enhanced.

The responsibility for guiding our children toward constructive use of their time is a big one. It is often difficult to tread the line between having bored children and pushing them too hard. This is where we feel our book can be enormously useful. Contests and creative opportunities, if pursued appropriately, can help make this time novel and exciting. At the same time, they will foster creativity, problem solving, exploration, experimentation, and mastery of skills.

Some adults, we realize, dislike the concept of contests for children. There are those who believe that competing is not natural or productive for children of this age. We feel, however, that the approach we have taken in this book answers these concerns. We encourage children to engage in those contests that are geared to their interests, whether it be photography, dance, computers, or science, and that give them an opportunity to excel. For growth to occur, though, adults and children must remember that it is the process of participating, rather than the winning or losing, that is most important.

Consider what it means to a child to engage successfully in an activity such as building a sandcastle, making a personal best in a music competition, growing and exhibiting the biggest or tiniest pumpkin with pride, designing a beautiful and original Mother's Day card, or creating an innovative model rocket or car. The sense of pride, self-confidence, and excitement that come from such experiences is best expressed by the children who wrote to us about their involvement in these activities:

> *"I thought building a mousemobile for the Odyssey of the Mind contest would be easy....It wasn't. A couple of times our team was really down in the dumps. We helped each other and came up with a workable design."*

> *"I liked the contest because it was an art contest and I like to draw robots. The theme was 'Computers and the Future.' It also gave me a chance to win something for myself and something for my school.*
>
> *My father and I read the contest rules very carefully. Then the whole family talked about ideas....Then I started by drawing. I tried to follow the contest rules so I would have a chance to win."*

> *"When I won, I was shocked! But, I was very happy and even proud to actually see my own story and name in print. I had a feeling (and still do) that it was only the beginning. Many more opportunities could just be waiting for the right moment."*

> *"It was one of the most memorable and beneficial things I have done so far in my life and will probably be for the rest of my life."*

These comments sum up beautifully for us exactly what contesting is all about. We hope that your children's experiences will be equally rewarding.

Joan Bergstrom

Craig Bergstrom

CHAPTER 1

Getting Started

Off to a Great Start

Today in the United States there are hundreds of contests kids your age can enter. You can also compete to get a book you've written published, or have a story or poem or drawing accepted by a magazine. What a thrill it would be to see your name in print and maybe even get a check in the mail for your efforts!

In the chapters that follow we describe all sorts of contests and publishing opportunities for you. We hope you'll flip through the book and find one or two you'd like to try right away. If you find a lot of contests that interest you, you might mark them somehow (maybe with stick-on dots) as a reminder to yourself. This will help you plan ahead for contests that are held at different times of the year.

Another way to find contests is by answering the questions in "How Do I Choose a Contest?" on pages 7–11. Take a look.

Tips for Entering a Contest

Before you actually enter a contest, please read this section. It should increase your chances of winning.

- Make sure you have a complete list of contest rules and eligibility requirements. If not, send for them. Be sure to include a self-addressed, stamped envelope.
- Anytime you write the sponsor, copy the address exactly as it's written in this book or on the entry form you get. If you fail to use the whole address when you're writing to large organizations, your mail could get lost. Don't forget the zip code, and be sure to put your return address on the envelope. Use the right amount of postage, too.
- Check to see if there's an entrance fee and make sure it's reasonable for you. Find out if there are additional fees if you advance to the next level in the contest.

- See if the contest is for groups or for individuals. Decide if you'd like to work alone or with a group. Working in a group can be fun and lets you learn from others, but you have to be willing to make compromises.
- Be sure you're really eligible to enter the contest.
- Correct your work. Neatness and accuracy count. You might want to get an adult to help you with this. Check your spelling, grammar, and punctuation. Typewritten material is great. If you must write it by hand, print it in ink, and be sure it can be read easily.
- Don't decorate your entry unless the rules ask for it.
- Go to the library and look at or read entries from past contests. Contest books and contest magazines are available for you to study. Check to see if your library has them. Also, read magazines and newspapers, look at former winners' art or photographs, and study the style of local winners in music or sports competitions.
- Include any required forms, box tops, or fees.
- For creative writing contests or photography and art, sending a self-addressed, stamped envelope is necessary if you want your work returned.
- If there is a closing date or a deadline, you must get your entry postmarked by midnight of that date. To be safe, get it to the post office before it closes. Otherwise, your entry might never be looked at.
- Consider entering contests that are for people of all ages. Many kids your age have won these contests.
- If you enter a contest that calls for creativity, judges will look for the following:

    Appropriateness: Your work must fit the subject.

    Sincerity: Your work must be believable. Talk about what you know in language everyone can understand.

    Clarity: Your work must be clear.

    Originality: To be original, you must avoid the obvious. If you don't think you have very unusual ideas, try letting your imagination go. Record all your thoughts. Try out your ideas with a friend, a teacher, a parent, or even your pets.

- If you get bogged down, talk to adults or other kids about your situation and problems. Sometimes even people who don't know much about contests call help you.
- Be patient. It's hard to wait, but judging takes time.
- Don't get discouraged if you don't win. Knowing you gave it

your best shot will be your reward for now. There will be other contests, and you will get better all the time.

- When you win, take the time to write and thank the sponsors and tell them what the experience meant to you.

Winning and Losing

We know for sure that some kids shouldn't enter contests. They are already involved in competition at school and everywhere else. For them one more contest or competitive sport would be too much. Contests, you know, are supposed to be fun. If you feel really nervous about entering any contest—don't!

However, if you're just a little nervous but think you would like to try, search out a contest you can do quietly and comfortably at home either by yourself or with a friend. There are many that won't drive you up a wall.

Are contests and competitions good for you? Some grown-ups don't think so. They think children shouldn't compete for prizes or rewards. They feel that children should only get involved in a project because it interests them or because they learn something special from it. They insist most kids are not at their creative best when they are competing for an award.

On the other hand, some grown-ups support contests and believe that many children love to enter them. They feel that kids do their very best work when they are competing with other kids. They believe that children do need rewards and that contests with rewards represent a realistic world for a child. They also believe there should be more than one prize for every contest. We agree.

Many children your age really like the excitement of competing against other children. They like to take risks and find that rough-and-tumble, hands-on contests are exciting for them.

Other kids feel there is too much attention given to contests in sports and sporting events. They are glad there are contests in other things such as art, photography, writing, and dancing, and they have a chance to be good at something, too.

But please remember, no matter what kind of contest you enter—doing your best is what is important. And, if you do your best, you're bound to have fun. As Bill Koch, winner of an Olympic medal in cross-country skiing, said: "Winning isn't everything. Striving for excellence is—it's the trying and caring that are important—winning is a bonus."

Remember, too, it's always better to be busy entering a contest than slouching around in front of the TV feeding your face and watching soaps or cartoons. What kind of life is that for a smart kid like you? Please let this book help you start something new or get better at something you already do. We wrote this book for you because we believe that if you enter the right contests you will not only have fun but you will also learn many interesting, new things. And, who knows? You may start a lifelong hobby for yourself and other members of your family.

Our Contests

This is the third edition of **All the Best Contests for Kids.** In each edition we run our own special contests for readers. The little creatures hiding all over the book have been there since the beginning. In the first edition, we ran a contest to name them. Jennifer Helfand suggested the name Fuzzdips, and we liked that. In every edition, we run a contest to find all the Fuzzdips. Everyone who enters will get a special Fuzzdip Finder certificate. If you find all the Fuzzdips, you'll win a special prize.

In the last edition of **All the Best Contests for Kids,** we offered the Design-a-Cover Contest. We challenged our readers to design a cover for this, the third edition of **All the Best Contests for Kids.** Christopher Burkhardt of New Orleans, Louisiana, won for the picture of the Fuzzdip that appears on this cover.

Honorable mention went to Tracy Greenberg of Ambler, Pennsylvania, Erin Donohue of Centerville, Virginia, and David Tamaki of Cresskill, New Jersey. There were so many good entries that it was tough to choose.

In the first edition, we asked kids to Design-a-Contest. Sharon Magee of Guilderland, New York, won first prize for her contest, Flags for Outer Space, in which children design flags for outer space colonies and explain what they mean.

Second place went to Sarah Straude of Watertown, Wisconsin. Her contest was Can You Make the Weirdest-Looking, Funniest Pizza? Contestants design strange, but still edible, pizzas.

Jennifer Cleland from Sacramento, California, won third prize for the All-American Birthday Contest. Contestants design everything for a party, from invitations to food.

Fourth prize was the Design-a-Skateboard Contest. Matthew Grande of Oyster Bay, New York, asked kids to create colorful designs for skateboards.

Maleka Kamara of Washington, D.C., won third prize for the Youth Nail Contest. Participants design special paintings or designs for fingernails.

We Need Reporters

We love to hear from our readers. To get all the information for you that this book contains, we wrote to more than 2,000 individuals and organizations and asked them if they sponsored contests or writing opportunities for kids 6 to 12. Here is a partial list of the groups or businesses that we contacted:

- Local and state departments of tourism
- State fair associations
- National organizations for children
- Children's and family magazines
- Hundreds of newspapers
- Companies that we know sponsor contests
- Music organizations
- Computer organizations
- Science organizations
- Mathematics organizations
- Mind-game societies
- Sports organizations

We got lots of answers from people and organizations on this list, but we also know there are hundreds, maybe thousands, of contests that we haven't heard about yet, contests that are different than the ones we've already listed. This is why we need kid reporters like you. We need you to tell us about contests and opportunities to get published. We plan to write a fourth edition of this book within the next year using information from you, our reporters. The next edition will then be yours, because many of your ideas and other kids' ideas will be in it. So be sure to write to us about any contests or opportunities for getting published that we should know about.

To help you in your reporting, check with your school teacher, coach, librarian, music or dance teacher, and your parents and grandparents. There may be some contests and chances to get published that only they know about.

You may also get information from bulletin boards at schools, community centers, libraries, museums, recreation centers, or nature centers. Your local newspaper might have notices that will be of interest to you. Be sure to check whenever you can.

Here is a form that we need you to follow in order to include your contest or writing opportunity in the next edition.

- Name of contest or chance to be published
- Sponsoring organization
- Address (street, city, state, zip code)

- Eligibility: Ages and special qualifications
- Time of year
- Information on contest or opportunity to be published: description; rules. If there is more than one level, describe how you get from the local to the national level.
- Where to get more information about it
- Prizes
- Your thoughts about the contest
- Your name
- Your address (street, city, state, zip code)

As we were writing the book, we also wrote to many children and asked them several questions about the contests that they had entered or the ways in which their work had been published. Many wrote us and told us how they got started, what they liked best about the activity, and the way they felt about their experiences. If you've had an interesting experience in a contest or writing activity, we'd like to hear from you, too. Here's the form that we need you to follow in order to include your words of wisdom in the next edition.

- Your name
- Your address (street, city, state, zip code)
- Your telephone number (include area code)
- Your parent's signature approving the use of your name
- Name of the contest or publication and official sponsor
- Your answers to the following questions:
  1. What do you think we should tell other kids about this activity?
  2. How did you find out about the contest or publication?
  3. What did you like best about it?
  4. How did you feel after it was over? What did you learn?
  5. Can you tell us how you got started in the activity?
  6. How old were you when you participated?
  7. How old are you now?

If we publish your idea and/or words of wisdom, we will send you a copy of the next edition and your name will be in print. We hope we will get so many replies that this book will be jam-packed with words of wisdom from kids all over the United States. We want to hear from you!

How Do I Choose a Contest?

This is a section for you if you are having trouble finding a good contest to enter. To help you decide what contests would be best for you, we have prepared some questions for you to answer. Answering them might help you learn more about yourself, your interests, and your abilities—and, after all, this is where you should really begin. It is best to enter contests that go along with your favorite activities, hobbies, special interests, or sports. Here are the questions we want you to ask yourself:

Question #1: *What Do I Really Like to Do? What Would I Like to Get Better At?*

The chart "What's Fun? What's Fabulous?" in the Appendix will help you to think about the kinds of activities you like to do best. You may be able to use this information to find a contest that will be just right for you. For instance, if you like horses and are good at photography, it would make good sense for you to enter one or two of your best horse pictures in a photography contest.

Is there an activity that you like but aren't very good at? Maybe a contest could help you improve. You could get some experience and work on your skills—just don't get upset if things don't work out as well as you'd like. If nothing interests you right away, look at another chart in the Appendix called "Yes, No, and Maybe." It lists over 250 activities that we found kids your age really like to do. Take the time to fill it out. As you do, you might enjoy putting stick-on dots beside the activities that you enjoy most. Then, as you read this book, look for contests that include these favorite activities. You could also put stick-on dots beside the contests you might want to enter. On the other hand, you might want to try something new. What do you find on the chart that appeals to you? Do you like to grow things? If you do, how about entering a 4-H crops program? If you like to paint, maybe a create-a-T-shirt contest is for you. If you like to draw and to write, then maybe you'd like to enter a greeting card–making contest.

Another way to help you think about things that you'd really like to do is to draw big pictures of the way you think you would look skiing, skating, baton twirling, rope jumping, or playing a clarinet. For example, if you find that you're always drawing pictures of yourself dressed in beautiful clothes and looking great, then maybe a fashion or sewing contest is for you.

Question #2: *What Materials, Equipment, and Musical Instruments Have Special Meaning for Me?*

Do materials like sketch pads, paint, clay, yarn, wood, fabric, or magic kits turn you on? What do you like to work with most? If you like doing magic tricks and you know you're getting good at them, you might want to audition to enter a talent show. If you like to use woodworking tools, maybe either a soapbox-car race or kite-making contest would be perfect for you. Is there a musical instrument that you play well? Do you think you'd like to play your trumpet in an audition for the all-county band?

When it comes to contesting, your own interests and the things you like to do best are your strength. Putting them to work for you may help you bring home a prize. But if they don't, think of how much fun you've had. And think how much you've learned.

Question #3: *What Animals Do I Like Best?*

If you have a pet, you already know how important it is for you to feed, exercise, play with, and clean your pet. Do you enjoy doing these things? Do you think this interest could lead you to a contest that has meaning for you? Can you, for example, imagine dressing up your dog in a pumpkin costume and entering her in a contest? What about putting your guinea pig on a special diet to improve his coat so you can enter him in a 4-H event at the state fair? If rabbits are your favorite, you might want to try entering a rabbit show.

Question #4: *Do I Like to Challenge My Brain?*

Are you interested in codes, puzzles, map reading, chess, and other games that challenge your mind? Do you like to create unusual things by yourself or with your friends? Do you find that creative problem-solving really excites you? If the answer to most of these questions is "yes," then you might want to enter a contest with other kids in which you have to think in new ways to solve problems. For example, in some contests teams of kids identify the contents of various boxes using all of their senses except sight.

If you are good at spelling and do well at school spelling bees, you may decide to practice hard so that you can go to the local spell-off as a representative of your school. If you study hard enough, when you're asked to spell words like "loganberry" and "locomotion" or maybe even "supercalifragilisticexpialidocious," you won't be stumped.

Question #5: *Do I Like to Read about Funny and Far-Out Things and Talk to People Who Do Them?*

Do you have a pet rock? Does the thought of making duck calls start your brain going? If so, then maybe you should get into some offbeat contest that really appeals to you. You may want to convince your family to go with you to the Tom Sawyer Fence Painting Contest in Hannibal, Missouri, or to the Pumpkin Fair contest in Morton, Illinois. Actually, there are hundreds of unusual contests all around the country. We describe a lot of them in chapter 5, "Far-Out Contests and Fabulous Fairs." And don't forget, you could even invent one of your own!

Question #6: *Do I Like to Write Stories, Letters, Advertisements, Plays, Poems, Books, and Jokes? Do I Like to Create Mazes, Puzzles, and Pictures?*

Does everyone you write letters to like to get them? Do you find that every time you write a story your teacher thinks it's wonderful? Do other kids love the puzzles you create? Maybe you should consider trying to get your best work published. Think about how great you'd feel when you see your article, column, or book in print. As people read your work you'll soon realize that they appreciate your opinion and creativity. Many children have published books and talk about how thrilled they were to see the final version with pictures and text—a task that took many hours and much rewriting.

When you read the section on getting your name in print, you'll discover there are many children's and family magazines and newspapers that offer you opportunities to see your work published. There are also groups that publish books written by children. If you read chapter 6, you'll learn how to go about doing it.

Question #7: *Do I Like to Create Ads, Posters, Sculptures, and Paintings?*

Do you spend tons of free time drawing, painting, printmaking, doing rubbings, making collages, and sculpting? Do you like studying the landscape around you? Well then, various kinds of art and visual contests may be the ones for you. There really are many opportunities to enter your work in art project contests. Be on the lookout for them at local museums and fairs and in magazines and newspapers.

Question #8: *What Is My Favorite Sport? Who Are the Sports Figures I Admire Most?*

What do sports mean to you? Do you find yourself playing the same sport all afternoon and on weekends, too? Has your coach or gym teacher complimented you on the way you play a game? If so, you might consider entering a contest in some sport you love or are especially good at.

Or maybe there's a sport you've never tried but think you might like. How about figure skating? Do you find yourself watching skaters on TV or begging your parents to take you to ice shows? Would you be willing to work alone for hours on figure eights, carefully tracing your own pattern over and over? Could you take it if you fell down many times trying to learn a jump? If your answer to questions like these is "yes," then figure skating could be a great sport for you.

On the other hand, you might do better working with a team. We know that some kids find it much harder to work alone than with a team or group of kids who practice together on an individual sport. Figure skating, biking, or running alone may be harder for you than doing those things with other people. Also, it's often much harder to track down the right competition alone and to get back and forth to events if you don't have anyone to go with.

Question #9: *Do I Like to Work in Groups?*

You can enter some contests with other people. Sometimes hard projects are more fun if you have the team spirit that comes from working in a group. Working in a group is a great chance to learn from other kids. You can also make new friends who are interested in things you like. If you want to enter a contest with other people, look for contests that allow this.

Now that you've thought about your interests, start by looking in the chapter that includes them. For example, if you like computers and problem solving, then chapter 3, "Crunching Numbers, Mind Games, and Other Trips Out," will probably be just for you. If your main interest is in getting published, then you should go straight to chapter 6, "Creating: Getting Your Name in Print."

Have fun, and remember, being in the contest—not winning or losing—is most important. If you do win, take the time to write and thank the contest sponsors and tell them what winning meant to you. Good luck!

Cracking the Codes

Each one of the contests or publishing opportunities begins with one or more picture symbols. With these pictures, you can tell at a glance just what the prizes are.

 = Money

This includes savings bonds, gift certificates, trust funds, scholarships, and, of course, cash.

 = Name in print

This means your name and sometimes your work will be published in a magazine, newspaper, newsletter, or book. If you write a play, it could be performed.

 = Glory

This includes recognition on TV or radio, being part of an awards ceremony, and also trophies, plaques, ribbons, medals, and certificates.

 = Gifts

This includes gifts for you, sometimes gifts for an adult who helped you, and sometimes gifts for your school or the local organization.

 = Trips

This includes trips for you and sometimes your parents, friends, a teacher, or a club leader.

 = Question mark

This means the prizes change from year to year.

Note: We have made every effort to be sure that information on the contests and publications included in this book is as accurate and up-to-date as possible. Few contests are run in exactly the same way year after year, though, and prizes and categories often change. Names and addresses may change, too. Please let us know if any of our information is incorrect or out of date.

CHAPTER 2

Creating  and Putting on the Hits

Annual National PTA Reflections Program—Visual Arts Category

Reflections Program
Visual Arts Category
National PTA
700 North Rush Street
Chicago, IL 60611

WHO CAN ENTER?

Open to students in schools that have an active PTA or PTSA. Students may enter in the following categories:
Primary: Kindergarten–Grade 3
Intermediate: Grades 4–6
Junior High School: Grades 7–9
Senior High School: Grades 10–12

TIME OF YEAR:

State contests: January through March
National contests: April

WHAT IS IT?

Students create artwork—drawings, paintings, collages, prints—based on a special theme set by the National PTA.

Have you been drawing pictures ever since you were 4 years old? Have you ever thought you would like to be an artist? Have you ever looked at a picture someone else has done and said: "I could do better than that!" Well, here's your chance. The Annual National PTA Reflections Theme Program in visual arts makes it possible for you to create a piece of art that will let you express your feelings and thoughts, and maybe win a prize for it.

Your artwork can be drawing, painting, collage, or printmaking. Ask your school's PTA about participating in Reflections. Only students enrolled in a PTA school may submit entries. Talk to your parents or teacher to help make certain your artwork qualifies according to the National PTA's definitions.

The rules that the National PTA has for drawings, paintings, collages, and printmaking:

1. Drawing: Crayon, chalk, charcoal, pencil, ink, or any other medium used for drawing or sketching may be used.
2. Painting: Any appropriate paint, including tempera, oil, and watercolor, may be used.
3. Collage: Whatever materials are deemed suitable by art teachers may be used. However, care should be exercised to assure that the collage composition is put together securely enough to travel well. Some collage compositions are not recommended for mailing because of rough handling in the mail and the effects of climatic changes.
4. Printmaking: All graphic processes—linoleum cuts, serigraphs, and etchings—are eligible.
5. Needlework: Any original design.

The rules for the contest are:

1. Artwork may be no larger than 24 inches by 30 inches overall, including mat.
2. Visual arts entries must be unframed but must be mounted on material suitable for display.
3. Nonwinning visual arts entries will be returned by the summer of the year you enter.
4. A parent must sign the entry form stating that the work submitted is original and done by one person only. Also, you must sign the permission release on the entry form.
5. Artwork done by two or more students will not be accepted in the visual arts division. However, a contestant may submit more than one piece of creative work.

Each year the Reflections program has a different theme. All entries in the visual arts division must relate to and express the year's special theme. (If your artwork does not express or relate to the special theme, then you must use the theme in the title or subtitle of your artwork.) For example, the theme in 1984–1985 was "What Sparks My Imagination," and the Outstanding Interpretation Award was granted to a child who drew a bright, lively picture of clouds in the sky. The 1991–1992 theme is "Exploring New Beginnings."

Submit your artwork to your local PTA/PTSA in the visual arts division. If your work is selected to go on to the district PTA, you may become one of the five state winners. You are notified, and your work is then submitted to the National PTA. At the national level your work is judged by a team of people who have design and art backgrounds.

Remember, you may also enter other pieces of your creative work in the other PTA arts contests described elsewhere in this book: photography, music, and literature.

PRIZES:

There are a total of three cash awards given at each level. In addition, each year there are also approximately 10 honorable mentions awarded.

First Place winners: $300

Second Place winners: $200

Third Place winners: $100

Outstanding Interpretation Award: A trip to the National PTA Convention accompanied by one adult, $250 scholarship, gold-plated Reflections Medallion

Honorable Mentions: Silver Reflections Medallions and art supplies. All entries reaching the national level receive Reflections Certificate of Participation and a book is given to their school library in their name.

Winners are announced at the National PTA Convention and through the PTA magazine and newsletters. The winning artwork entries are shown in the National PTA Traveling Exhibit. This exhibit travels throughout the United States.

WHAT ARE MY CHANCES?

Last year, there were 256 students who made it to the national level. There were 12 winners and 40 honorable mentions.

Crayola National Coloring Event

P.O. Box 598
Easton, PA 18044-0598

WHO CAN ENTER?

Ages 7 and under
Ages 8–12

TIME OF YEAR:

Entries are accepted from June 1–October 31

WHAT IS IT?

Kids create pictures, paintings, or three-dimensional constructions based on a theme. In 1989 the theme of the Coloring Event was "Share Your World." Kids were asked to show the people, places, and activities that make up their world. The pictures and creations kids submitted were of their neighborhoods and schools and of secret and imaginary places.

1989 PRIZES:

Grand Prize in each category: $25,000 college scholarship
500 First Prizes: Five-foot-tall Crayola crayon replica
750 Second Prizes: Adidas Backpacks
1,000 Third Prizes: Adidas Fun Balls
Everyone who enters receives a poster.

For an entry form, send a self-addressed, stamped envelope to Crayola National Coloring Event, P.O. Box 598, Easton, PA 18044-0598.

MADD National Youth Programs (Mothers Against Drunk Driving) Poster Contest

MADD National Youth Programs
P.O. Box 541688
Dallas, TX 75354-1688

WHO CAN ENTER?

Grades 1–3
Grades 4–6
Grades 7–9
Grades 10–12

TIME OF YEAR:

Local contests: Time varies
Individual entry judging: March
National contest judging: March

WHAT IS IT?

A poster contest that focuses on the problem of drinking and driving.

This contest is your chance to be both an artist and a teacher. As an artist, you will draw a poster that you think best shows the meaning of the contest theme. For example, one year the theme was "Drunk Drivers Destroy Dreams." The artists in this contest designed posters that went with that theme.

Your poster design will help educate other kids and adults about the importance of safe driving and the dangers of drinking and driving. In the United States today, drinking and driving is one of the leading causes of death. The message you create through your design will be your lesson to others.

You may use any medium: water color, oil, crayon, acrylic, pencil, ink, magic marker, or collage.

The rules for the contest are:

1. The poster must be no smaller than 11 inches by 17 inches and no larger than 16 inches by 20 inches.
2. The following information must appear on the back of each poster. Entries lacking this information will be automatically disqualified.

- Name, age, address, telephone number of participant
- Social Security number of child or parent
- Name and telephone number of MADD chapter submitting entry
- Grade division for which the poster is entered
- A signed permission slip must be attached to each entry stating that the MADD National Office has the participant's permission to use the poster for publicity purposes

3. Once local winners have been selected, the first-place winners in each division are forwarded to the MADD National Office. The local office is responsible for seeing that the posters arrive in good condition, and to do this they have to pack the winning entries in sturdy containers.

If there is no local MADD organization through which you can submit your entry, you will need to write the National Office for instructions. They will tell you how to enter the "Individual Entry" contest. If you win the "Individual Entry" contest, your winning entry is entered into the national contest. If you are part of a group, such as a school group or a scout troop, the first-prize winners from your group should be mailed to the MADD National Office for judging in the national contest. Your leader can write for the guidelines.

PRIZES:

Local contests
Prizes decided upon locally

National "Individual Entry" contest
First Prize: $100 and plaque
Second Prize: $50 and plaque
Third Prize: $25 and plaque

National contests
First Prize for each grade division: $1,000, trophy, and all-expense-paid trip to New York City with a chaperone for an awards ceremony sponsored by the National Highway Traffic Safety Administration
Second Prize for each grade division: $500 and plaque
Third Prize for each grade division: $250 and plaque

WHAT ARE MY CHANCES?

In 1988, 45,000 people entered. There were 18 individual winners and 21 national winners.

Morgan Horse Art Contest

The American Morgan Horse Association, Inc.
P.O. Box 960
Shelburne, VT 05482

WHO CAN ENTER?

Ages 13 and younger
Ages 14–21
Adult

TIME OF YEAR:

January

WHAT IS IT?

You create a design that features the Morgan horse. There are three separate contests: Morgan Art, Morgan Cartoons, and Morgan Specialty Pieces. Art can include art forms such as pencil sketches, watercolors, oils, or sculptures. Morgan Cartoons include people, horses, and jokes in cartoon form. Morgan Specialty Pieces include sculpture and carvings.

Morgan horses have a special place in the history of our country. During the pioneer days the Morgan was the favorite riding horse. Some people believe that the Morgan was more faithful, longer-lasting, stronger, and more lovable than what we use today—the automobile.

The Morgan Horse Art Contest is a chance for you to discover something about history and horses. If you don't know much about Morgan horses, you can write for a brochure and pictures from the Morgan Horse Association. Or you could do a little research at the library. You can find lots of pictures of Morgan horses and stories about people who have owned Morgans in the past.

You may enter as many art pieces as you want. A $2 entry fee must accompany each piece. Entries for each category will be judged on creativity, artistic quality, originality, breed promotion, and overall appearance. Some entries may be used for promotional purposes. For example, the organization may use your entry to sell certain gift items. They also might use it in the *Morgan Horse* magazine along with a story. Entries will not be returned.

PRIZES:

First Place in each age category: $50
Top five places in Morgan Art, Cartoons, and Specialty Pieces: Ribbons

Ocean Pals

c/o Beneath The Sea
P.O. Box 644
Rye, NY 10580

WHO CAN ENTER?

Kindergarten–Grade 6
Grades 7–12

TIME OF YEAR:

January

WHAT IS IT?

Kids create posters about a special undersea theme. Ocean Pals are concerned kids—these kids show how all creatures should be able to live beneath the sea.

If you've been to the beach, you know how yucky it is when the ocean isn't clean. Many people are concerned about pollution, and a group of scuba divers decided to try to do something about it. They sponsor Ocean Pals to help kids think about how important a clean ocean is. To enter Ocean Pals, you should make a poster that shows the theme of the year, which will be about a clean ocean. The 1990 theme was "Our friends beneath the sea want a clean home, too."

You should draw or paint your poster on 16" × 24" unruled and unlined paper. It can be color or black and white; just make sure that it won't smudge. Attach the entry form to the back and mail it rolled up in a tube.

Good luck helping to keep the oceans clean!

PRIZES:

Vary from year to year

Annual National PTA Reflections Program—Music Category

National PTA
700 North Rush Street
Chicago, IL 60611-2571

WHO CAN ENTER?

Open to students in schools that have an active PTA or PTSA. There are four levels:

Primary: Kindergarten–Grade 3
Intermediate: Grades 4–6
Junior High School: Grades 7–9
Senior High School: Grades 10–12

TIME OF YEAR:

State contests: January through March
National contests: April

WHAT IS IT?

Students create musical pieces, with or without words, based on a special theme set each year by the National PTA.

Does music inspire you? Does it make you tap your feet or hum along? Then maybe this program is for you. Maybe you should try your hand at writing some music—anything from a simple tune to an elaborate symphony piece.

Your musical piece can be written with or without words. It can be for someone to sing or to play on a musical instrument. Ask your school's PTA about participating in Reflections. Talk to your parents or a teacher to help make certain your musical piece qualifies according to the National PTA's rules.

The rules for the contest are:
1. Musical scores, with or without words, are acceptable. However, both words and music must be the original work of the submitting entrant.

2. The composition must be submitted on standard music manuscript paper appropriate for the instrumentation or voicing (nonspiral sides). Primary and Intermediate divisions don't need to submit notation, but must submit a cassette.
3. Single-sheet entries may be mounted, if desired, on any suitable material such as poster paper or lightweight cardboard. No entry, regardless of the form in which it is submitted, should be more than 11 by 14 inches overall.
4. Copies of the student's original work are acceptable; the student is encouraged to keep the original or a copy of the entry. Music entries will not be returned.
5. It is strongly recommended that a tape of the composition be submitted along with the manuscript. Cassette-type tapes are recommended because they greatly assist the judges in making final selections. (Cassettes should be in their own plastic or cardboard sleeves, identified, and packaged with the entry blank and manuscript in a large envelope.)
6. Words written to music already published are not acceptable.
7. A composition by two or more students will not be accepted. However, an entrant may submit more than one composition.
8. A parent must sign the entry form stating that the work submitted is original and done by one person only. Also, you must sign the permission release on the entry form.

Each year the Reflections program has a different theme. For example, the theme for 1991–1992 is "Exploring New Beginnings." All entries must relate to and express the year's theme. If your musical composition does not express or relate to the special theme, then you must use the theme in the title or subtitle of your work.

Submit your musical composition to your local PTA/PTSA. If your work is selected to go on to the district PTA, you may become one of the five state winners. You are notified, and your work is then submitted to the National PTA. At the national level, your work is judged by a team of people who have a musical background.

You may also enter other pieces of your creative work in the other PTA arts categories described elsewhere in this book: visual arts, photography, and literature.

PRIZES:

There are a total of three cash awards given at each level. In addition, each year there are also approximately 10 honorable mentions awarded.

First Place: $300

Second Place: $200

Third Place: $100

Outstanding Interpretation Award: An expense-paid trip to the National PTA Convention accompanied by one adult, $250 scholarship, gold-plated Reflections Medallion

Honorable Mentions: Silver-plated Reflections Medallion

All entrants reaching the national level receive a Reflections Certificate of Participation, and a book is donated to their school library in their name.

Winners are announced at the National PTA Convention and through the PTA magazine and newsletters. Outstanding Interpretation winner will perform for the delegates at the convention.

BMI Music Awards to Student Composers

Ralph N. Jackson
BMI Student Composer Awards
320 West 57th Street
New York, NY 10019

WHO CAN ENTER?

The competition is open to students who are citizens or permanent residents of the Western Hemisphere, including North, Central, and South America and the Caribbean Island nations, and who are enrolled in accredited secondary schools, colleges, or conservatories or are studying privately with recognized and established teachers anywhere in the world. Contestants must be under 26 years of age.

TIME OF YEAR:

February 10 each year

WHAT IS IT?

The contest is designed to encourage young composers in the creation of concert music and, through cash prizes, to aid in continuing their musical education.

Do you ever compose music when you're practicing your piano or clarinet? Do you compose for your music theory lessons? If you do, maybe you should ask your teacher to go over your composition and then enter it in the BMI Music Awards to Student Composers.

Today, BMI is the largest musical licensing organization in the world. More than 50% of the music played on American radio stations in the past year is licensed by BMI. Each year BMI sponsors a variety of workshops and seminars designed to encourage participation in all areas of music.

Over the last 37 years, 346 students from 8 to 25 years old have received BMI awards. For the competition, there are no limitations as to instrumentation, stylistic consideration, or length of work submitted. However, students may enter only one composition.

PRIZES:

Range from $500 to $2,500

WHAT ARE MY CHANCES?

In 1989, over 400 people submitted compositions, and 16 winners were chosen.

National Children's Whistling Championship

Franklin County Arts Council
P.O. Box 758
Louisburg, NC 27549

WHO CAN ENTER?

Children: Ages 12 and under
Teenage: Ages 13–19

TIME OF YEAR:

Local contests: Throughout the year
National convention: April

WHAT IS IT?

A convention where whistlers from all over the country can compete.

The National Whistling Convention has contests, concerts, and workshops for whistlers, including kids. They emphasize whistling while you work or play. For the Children's Whistling Championship, contestants whistle one selection in each category. There are maximum times in each category: six minutes in classical, four minutes in popular, and four minutes in novelty. Those are maximums—selections should be shorter if possible. A panel of five judges will be selected by the Franklin County Arts Council on the basis of their knowledge of music or whistling or other special qualifications. The judges will rate contestants from 1 to 5 in three categories: ability, creativity, and performance. Ability is judged as talent, skill, and professional quality or potential. Creativity is inventiveness, artistry, and originality. Performance is audience appeal, stage presence, personal style, and attitude. Start whistling and good luck!

PRIZES:

First Place: Money, a trophy, and a ribbon
Second Place: Money, a trophy, and a ribbon
Honorable Mention: Ribbon for all participants

National Federation of Music Clubs Junior Festivals

National Federation of Music Clubs (NFMC)
1336 North Delaware Street
Indianapolis, IN 46202

WHO CAN ENTER?

Anyone up to 19 years of age by March 1 of the year of the festival. All participants must be members of NFMC, either as club members or as special members.

TIME OF YEAR:

February–April

WHAT IS IT?

Each State Federation in the National Federation of Music Clubs holds yearly festivals where students audition and win awards.

If you prepare carefully for the National Federation of Music Clubs Junior Festivals auditions, you could receive a Gold Cup. It takes three years of superior ratings to get a Gold Cup.

NFMC Junior Festivals are held in the 41 states where the Federation has active senior clubs. In 1991, 90,000 students participated in the festivals.

What is it like to go to an NFMC Junior Festival? The organization arranges for a festival site and sends notices to music teachers about the auditions. At the festival, individuals or groups audition before judges who are music teachers. The 21 categories include:

- Electronic organ
- Flute and flute ensemble
- Hand bells
- Hymn playing
- Piano (solo, duet for 4 hands, trio for 1 piano and 6 hands, duo for 2 pianos and 4 hands, quartet for 2 pianos and 8 hands)
- Violin
- Woodwinds
- Brass

Each individual or group plays two pieces. The first is an American composition, which each contestant is required to play. The required pieces are at different levels; you and your teacher can choose one that you will be able to play the best. In the second part of the audition you may choose whatever you want to play. Students are not judged against each other. Each participant is rated superior, excellent, very good, good, or fair.

In some states, dance auditions are held in ballet, theatre dance, and tap. Categories for the auditions are according to age.

PRIZES:

Superior ratings for three or more years: Gold Cup
Superior ratings for three consecutive years: Special certificates
All participants: Certificates of appreciation

The American Kennel Club (AKC) Junior Showmanship

The American Kennel Club
51 Madison Avenue
New York, NY 10010

WHO CAN ENTER?

Ages 10–16

TIME OF YEAR:

Any time an AKC dog show is held

WHAT IS IT?

At official AKC dog shows, kids 10 through 16 enter their purebred dogs to be judged. Judging may be based on how well the dog fits the standards for its breed or on how well trained the dog is (obedience trials). There are also Junior Showmanship classes in which judging is based solely on how well the dog handler shows the dog.

At the 1989 Westminster Kennel Club show (the Olympics of dog shows), a 16-year-old won the prize as top junior handler with her beautiful Doberman pinscher. Her win represented five years of hard work showing dogs and hours of work with her champion dog.

To get to the Westminster show, junior AKC members must win at least eight Junior Showmanship trophies in the preceding year. Since not all AKC shows have Junior Showmanship classes, you will have to check your local dog shows to see if participation in them will qualify you for national competition. There are a number of special rules that apply to junior competitions. You can learn about them from the people who run your local contests or you can send to the AKC for a rules booklet.

Since the American Kennel Club was founded to protect and improve purebred dogs, only those dogs registered with AKC can be entered in the official dog shows. AKC members have found that exhibiting their dogs in shows is a good way of showing progress made in breeding. Obedience and field trials help show improvements in the dogs' stamina and obedience. (Field trials are held outdoors, and, in these, dogs are judged on how well trained they are as hunting dogs.)

PRIZES:

First Prize: Rose Ribbon or Rosette
Second Prize: Brown Ribbon or Rosette
Third Prize: Light Green Ribbon or Rosette
Fourth Prize: Gray Ribbon or Rosette

Annual National PTA Reflections Program—Photography Category

National PTA
Reflections Program
700 North Rush Street
Chicago, IL 60611-2571

WHO CAN ENTER?

Open to students in schools that have an active PTA or PTSA. There are four levels:

Primary: Kindergarten–Grade 3
Intermediate: Grades 4–6
Junior High School: Grades 7–9
Senior High School: Grades 10–12

TIME OF YEAR:

State contests: January through March
National contests: April

WHAT IS IT?

Students take photographs based on a special theme set each year by the National PTA.

You don't need a fancy camera to have fun taking pictures. And you don't need a fancy camera to win a prize, either. Unusual photographs win awards. So do ordinary shots. Imagination is the key to good photography. Keep your eyes open for something different. Who knows what you may discover on a walk with your camera in your own neighborhood?

Your photographs can be pictures of practically anything, as long as they relate to the PTA's special theme. Ask your school's PTA about participating in Reflections.

The rules for the contest are:

1. Prints in either black and white or color will be accepted. Snapshots, including instant photos, are acceptable.

2. All prints must be mounted on materials suitable for display. Work including mat can be no larger than 11 inches by 14 inches. Work must be unframed.
3. Work should be copied before submission and negatives retained by the entrant. Instant prints will be returned if return is requested in writing on the back of the mounted work.
4. A parent must sign the entry form stating that the work submitted is original and done by one person only. Also, a permission release form must be completed.
5. Photography done by two or more students will not be accepted. However, an entrant may submit more than one print.

Each year the Reflections program has a different theme. All entries must relate to and express the year's theme. If your photography does not express or relate to the theme, then you must use the theme in the title or subtitle of your pictures. The 1990–1991 theme was "If I Had a Wish." The 1991–1992 theme is "Exploring New Beginnings."

Submit your photography to your local PTA/PTSA in the photography category. If your work is selected to go on to the district PTA, you may become one of the five state winners. You are notified, and your work is then submitted to the National PTA. At the national level, your work is judged by a team of people who have a photography background.

You may also enter other pieces of your creative work in the other PTA division programs as described elsewhere in this book.

PRIZES:

First Place winners: $300

Second Place winners: $200

Third Place winners: $100

Outstanding Interpretation Award: A trip to the national PTA convention with one adult guardian, a $250 scholarship, and a gold-plated Reflections medallion

Honorable Mentions: Silver-plated Reflections medallion

Winners are announced at the National PTA convention and through the PTA magazine and newsletters. The winning photography entries are shown in the National PTA Traveling Exhibit. This exhibit travels throughout the United States.

Kodak International Newspaper Snapshot Awards (KINSA)

The KINSA contest is cosponsored by Eastman Kodak Company and participating newspapers across North America. Contact your local newspapers to see if they participate. Do not contact Eastman Kodak about the contest unless you cannot get the information locally.

WHO CAN ENTER?

All ages; amateur photographers only

TIME OF YEAR:

KINSA is a summertime contest that opens early in May and runs through the end of August. A newspaper has to run its local contest for a minimum of six weeks during this time period. International judging is in October.

WHAT IS IT?

The KINSA contest offers amateur photographers local recognition for their photographic abilities, the possibility of international acclaim, and the lure of cash or travel prizes.

Imagine your winning picture displayed at the EPCOT Center and in exhibits around the country. Your photography will be seen and admired by many. Winning a KINSA contest would be a thrill you'd never forget. It might even make you think about becoming a professional photographer.

First, you enter a KINSA photo contest put on by your local newspaper. Chances are, if your picture reaches the finals of the local newspaper contest, your entry will be sent to Eastman Kodak Company for the international judging. Each participating newspaper can forward a total of eight entries to Kodak. These will compete with entries from other newspapers for the $45,000 in international prizes. To qualify for the international awards, entries must be taken on Kodak film.

To enter KINSA contest's international judging, you must send in the original negative or transparency when requested by the newspaper. Written permission from any people included in your photographs must also be obtained.

1990 PRIZES:

International Awards

Grand Award for Best of Show: A trip for two to the opening of the KINSA Exhibit at the EPCOT Center in Florida, a four-day passport for EPCOT/Magic Kingdom (Disney World), $300 spending money, and $10,000 (one award only, for either black and white or color)

First Place awards: A trip for two to the opening of the KINSA Exhibit at the EPCOT Center, a four-day passport for EPCOT/Magic Kingdom, $300 spending money, and $5,000 (one award for color, one for black and white)

Second Place awards: $3,000 (one award for color, one for black and white)

Third Place awards: $2,000 (one award for color, one for black and white)

50 Honor awards: $250 each

200 Special Merit awards: $50 each

Local Awards

Local awards are often cash or gift certificates and range from $1,000 for First Prize (all ages) to $50 for a special youth award. Prizes vary from community to community.

For more information, contact the newspaper nearest you participating in the KINSA contest.

What do you think we should tell other kids about the contest you won?

....

"When you enter a contest, don't say, 'Oh, I'll never win' or 'Probably everyone will do better than me'; just don't put yourself down."

Paul Calandrella

Morgan Horse Photography Contest

The American Morgan Horse Association
P.O. Box 960
Shelburne, VT 05482

WHO CAN ENTER?

Open to all ages. Open to amateur and professional photographers.
Special category for those 18 and under.

TIME OF YEAR:

December 1

WHAT IS IT?

Kids take photographs of Morgan horses based on a special theme
set each year by the American Morgan Horse Association.

If you love horses, this photography contest might be for you. If
you're interested in photography, too, then this contest is definitely
for you. By taking pictures of a Morgan horse you think is especially
handsome, you can do two things that interest you at the same time
and you might even win something for it.

Each year the American Morgan Horse Association selects a
special theme. Your photographs must relate to the year's special
theme. For example, the theme in 1991 is "Absolutely Morgan."
Other special rules include:

1. All photographs must be of a registered Morgan horse and be
   described with a caption.
2. Photographs may be color or black-and-white prints, 5 inches
   by 7 inches or 8 inches by 10 inches in size.
3. A $2 entry fee is required for each photograph submitted.
4. You may submit as many photographs as you wish. A separate entry form must be taped to the back of each photo you
   submit.
5. Mounting of photos is desirable, but not required.
6. Entries will not be returned. Winning photos may be used for
   promotional purposes by the American Morgan Horse Association. Duplicates of the photograph may be used by the
   photographer.

To enter the contest, you must submit your photo or photographs. They will be judged by a professional photographer. Photographs are judged on creativity, spontaneity of subject, technical quality, breed promotion, and overall appearance. Winning photography entries are published in *The Morgan Horse,* a national magazine, and are often used for promotional purposes.

PRIZES:

First Prize in Youth Category: $50
Second Prize in Youth Category: $25

World Footbag Association (WFA) Worlds Photo Contest

World Footbag Association
1317 Washington Avenue, Suite 7
Golden, CO 80401

WHO CAN ENTER?

All ages

TIME OF YEAR:

August 15 deadline

WHAT IS IT?

Photographers take pictures of footbag players in competition.

Camera buffs, bring out your hardware. Take pictures of footbag competitors in the following categories: footbag freestyle, footbag net, footbag consecutive, footbag golf, funniest picture, and female player. The WFA is looking for pictures of the incredible championship moments that can be preserved only through pictures. In addition to prizes, all winning photographs are featured in the magazine *Footbag World*.

There are a couple of rules for entering the contest:
1. All photographs submitted become the property of the WFA.
2. Photos must be 8-by-10-inch prints only (black-and-white prints preferred).

PRIZES:

First Prize in each category: WFA team shirt and shorts, lifetime WFA Membership, and a 32-panel Kanga Footbag

Crafts with Simplicity Contests

Consumer Relations
Simplicity Pattern Co., Inc.
200 Madison Avenue
New York, NY 10016

WHO CAN ENTER?

Any resident of the United States or Canada

TIME OF YEAR:

Look for the contests in the spring and fall issues of *Crafts with Simplicity.*

WHAT IS IT?

Kids, teenagers, or adults use their artistic skills to create sewing or crafts projects.

We bet there are clothes you'd love to wear that your parents refuse to buy or let you wear out of the house. Wouldn't you love to create a fantasy wardrobe from scratch? We are giving you the rules for the "Great Doll Cover-Up" contest, an example of the kind of contest that Simplicity has sponsored in the past. In the "Great Doll Cover-Up" contest, kids designed and created wardrobes for dolls they made using a basic pattern. The rules for the "Great Doll Cover-Up" contest were:

1. Entries had to be made exclusively of products from V.I.P. Fabrics, Wm. E. Wright Co., and Stacy Industries, Inc.
2. Each entry consisted of two dolls, five outfits (a total of seven pieces), a carrying case, an official entry form from *Crafts with Simplicity,* and proofs of purchase of the products used.
3. Contestants signed the entry form to indicate that their entries were their own creations. For those contestants under 18 years, a parent or guardian also signed the entry form.
4. More than one entry was permitted per contestant. A separate form had to accompany each entry.

5. Each doll had to be made of basswood from the pattern given.
6. The carrying case for the two dolls had to duplicate the one in the directions.
7. Contestants decided on the color and style of the hair. The hair did not have to be the same as the sample dolls.
8. Entries were sent by regular mail only.
9. Entries could not be returned. All entries were to be donated to the United States Marine Corps' Toys for Tots Program for distribution during the holiday season.
10. Winners of any prizes in the "Great Doll Cover-Up" contest gave Simplicity Pattern Co., Inc. the right to use their names, designs, and dolls for advertising, promotional, or editorial purposes.
11. No correspondence or telephone calls were accepted from contestants.

Entries were judged on the basis of originality, color selections and combinations, workmanship, and how closely contest rules were followed.

PRIZES:
First Prize: $500
Second Prize: $250
Third Prize: $100
Fourth–Sixth prizes: $50 each
Ten Runners-Up prizes: Basket of goodies from Stacy, V.I.P., and Wrights

National Make It Yourself with Wool Competition

1323 Elkhorn
Belle Fourche, SD 57717

WHO CAN ENTER?

There are three categories for children:
Preteen: Ages 13 and under
Junior: Ages 14–17
Senior: Ages 18–24

TIME OF YEAR:

National Finals: January

WHAT IS IT?

Create your own fashionable wool clothing.

Are you an expert knitter, sewer, or crocheter? You can show off homemade wool creations in the National Make It with Wool Competition.

- Preteens can enter wool jumpers, skirts, dresses, pants, vests, sweaters, jackets, or shirts.
- Juniors and seniors may enter dresses, coats, or skirts.

The rules of the contest are:
1. All those entering the competition must select, construct, and model the garment themselves. Contest entrants may have advisors, but the advisor, parent, or teacher cannot select, cut, press, sew, knit, or crochet the garment.
2. All entries must be made from loomed, knitted, or felted fabric or yarn of 100% wool or of a minimum of 60% wool and 40% synthetic fiber blend. When you buy fabric or yarn for your contest entry, make sure it is made of at least 60% wool.
3. Trimmings may be of fabrics other than wool or a 60/40 wool blend, but fabrics other than wool may not be used for entire sections of a garment (such as entire sleeves, panels, or inserts).
4. To be eligible for the contest, your wool garment must be completed by January 1 of the current year.

For more rules, write to the National Make It Yourself with Wool Competition.

PRIZES:

First Place Junior and Senior winners: $2,000 scholarship or a trip to New York City

Other prizes include: Scholarships; sewing, knitting, and serger machines and supplies; luggage; savings bonds; fabrics; and more.

Special prizes: Vary from year to year; have included a full four-year scholarship to Western Reserve University

WHAT ARE MY CHANCES?

Last year there were 300,000 entries nationwide and over 1,700 made it to the national finals. Prizes were awarded in 14 categories at each level of competition (district, state, and national).

Sew 'N Show Contest

The McCall Pattern Company
11 Penn Plaza #18
New York, NY 10001-2065

WHO CAN ENTER?

There are two age divisions:
Ages 14 and under
Ages 15–18

TIME OF YEAR:

May

WHAT IS IT?

Kids sew clothes using McCall's patterns.

Choosing fabric and a pattern to sew is like going to the candy store. There are so many colorful fabrics and stylish patterns you may want to buy them all. It is exciting to start a new sewing project. As you begin to sew, you may think of some creative touches to add to your entry, such as unusual buttons or fancy ribbon. Sometimes it is helpful to have a parent or teacher around when you sew, because if you get stuck or frustrated they can help you out. The best reward for all your hard work is being able to wear something new and knowing that you made it!

You can sew your project on your own, in school, or as part of a 4-H sewing project. When you sew your entry, remember to follow these rules:

1. You must use a McCall's pattern from the current *McCall's Catalog*.
2. You may submit only one entry.
3. Grand prize winners from past years cannot enter the contest again.
4. Entries must include one color photograph of you modeling the clothing you sewed, fabric swatches, the official entry form filled out completely, and a description of your entry.

You send the color photograph of your sewing project, fabric swatches, and the official entry form in May. Do not send the clothing you sewed. The judges will choose a total of 40 finalists from all photography entries, 20 from each age category. If you are one of the 40 finalists, you will be notified by telephone and asked to send the clothing you sewed to McCall's in June. The judges will choose two grand prize winners in each age category in June. Judging will be done by home-sewing experts based on the quality of construction, fabric use, and creativity.

1989 PRIZES:

Grand Prize in each age division: An all-expenses-paid trip to New York City for the winner and their teacher, leader, or chaperone. The trip included:

- Tickets to a Broadway show
- Beauty makeover at a New York salon
- A cruise around New York
- A wardrobe of McCall's garments and an assortment of accessories
- Your picture in the *McCall's Pattern Catalog, Fashion* magazine, and *Sew News* magazine.

Second Prize in each age division: An overlock/serger sewing machine

Third Prize in each age division: Ten certificates for McCall's patterns

In addition, the club, organization, or school that submits the most entries wins a sewing machine.

What do you think we should tell other kids about the contest you won?
....

"Just remember: If you want something bad enough, you can get it. GO FOR IT!!!"

Joy Croft

CHAPTER 3

Crunching Numbers, Mind Games, and Other Trips Out

Boston Public Schools/Aardvark Systems and Programming, Inc. Elementary, Middle, and High School Computer Competition

Office of Technology Development
The Humphrey Center
75 New Dudley Street
Boston, MA 02119

WHO CAN ENTER?

Boston Public School students in grades 3–12.
There are three age groups:
Grades 3–5: LOGOwriter Programming
Grades 6–8: LOGOwriter Programming; BASIC Programming;
Data Base
Grades 9–12: Spreadsheet Applications; BASIC and Pascal
Programming; Data Bases

TIME OF YEAR:

Registration in December
Competition in February

WHAT IS IT?

Teams of two to four children write computer programs.

When you work on computer programs as a team, you share your
passion for computers with other kids who are excited about computers, too. Together you can solve problems you couldn't solve
alone because you can help and cheer each other on. When you
win, you'll be able to celebrate your fame and glory with other kids.
If you lose, you won't feel so bad because you can share your
disappointment with your team.

The rules for the contest are:

1. A minimum of two and a maximum of four students may form a team.
2. A school may enter only one team.
3. If you enter this contest, you may not enter the other computer contests sponsored by the Boston Public Schools.
4. Each team must bring its own computer system.
5. Only one computer per team may be used, and teams are responsible for their own equipment.
6. All teams must be accompanied by a teacher.

On the contest day in February your team arrives, with a computer, at the Office of Technology. You will have 2½ hours to write computer programs worth 1 to 3 points each. Teams with the largest accumulated total points win.

PRIZES:

All contestants: Commemorative T-shirt
Top three school teams in each category: Trophies

Can you tell us how you got started in the activity?

....

"Well, we got started by talking about it."

Josephine Marrero

"I got started in it because it was a science project assigned by our second-grade teacher, Sr. Mary Deborah."

Sarah Eckert

Boston Public Schools/Aardvark Systems and Programming, Inc. Primary, Elementary, Middle, and High School Computer Competition

Office of Technology Development
The Humphrey Center
75 New Dudley Street
Boston, MA 02119

WHO CAN ENTER?

Boston Public School students in Kindergarten–Grade 12 are eligible. There are four age groups:

Grades K–2: Primary Story Writing

Grades 3–5: Elementary Story Writing; Graphics LOGOwriter

Grades 6–8: Graphics LOGOwriter; Graphics BASIC; Educational Games

Grades 9–12: Graphics BASIC and Pascal; Educational Games; Programming Applications

TIME OF YEAR:

March, April, May

WHAT IS IT?

Kids write stories, draw pictures, or create a new version of a game on a computer.

By now, you have written many stories at school and at home, but do you know that you can write a story on a computer? Writing a story on a computer is easier than writing one with pencil and paper. On a computer, you can change your mind, add new sentences, and correct your spelling mistakes without making a mess.

If you are a computer whiz, you might even write your own computer program for creating drawings or playing a game. You have probably played video games and thought, "Wouldn't it be great if we could change it to make it even more fun?" This is your chance to become a game expert, author, and artist all at the same time!

The rules for the contests are:

1. All contest entries must be your original work or program.
2. A little bit of help from your teacher is acceptable.
3. Your completed entry must include:
   - Your name, school, contest category, and the title of your program printed on the diskette label
   - A clearly labeled diskette that runs on either Apple IIe, Apple II+, Macintosh, IBM PCjr, or IBM Model 25 or 30
   - A printout of the program and directions for accessing and following the program (documentation)
   - A completed application form
   - A teacher's signature on the application form indicating that the entry is the work of the student
4. Boston Public Schools reserves the right to duplicate winning entries for internal distribution.
5. Students entering this contest may not enter the Boston Public Schools/Aardvark Systems and Programming, Inc. Computer Team Competition held in February.

There are also special rules in each contest category. Remember, the topics and story-starter sentences in the story-writing categories change from year to year.

Primary Story Writing (Kindergarten–Grade 2):

1. Your story must begin with this story-starter sentence: "My mother would let me keep a robot in our house because..."
2. A word-processing program must be used to complete the story starter.
3. Entries must be no longer than one double-spaced page.
4. A computer printout of the finished story must be sent.

Elementary Story Writing (Grades 3–5):

1. Your story must be on the following topic: "You have suddenly been given the power to program computers. They will carry out any instructions you give them. The only catch is that your program must improve the world. What program would you write? How will it change the world?"
2. A word-processing program must be used to complete the story topic.
3. Entries must be at least one double-spaced page and no longer than two double-spaced pages.
4. A computer printout of the finished story must be sent.

Story writing in both categories will be judged on:
- Appropriate use of word processing
- Creativity/originality

- Plot/story sequence
- Proper word usage such as grammar, spelling, punctuation, and vocabulary

LOGOwriter and BASIC Graphics (Grades 3–12):

1. Programs must be written in IBM or LOGOwriter or BASIC.
2. No other commercial program may be used in conjunction with LOGOwriter.
3. If you are in Grades 6–12, shape tables may be used for the Apple. No other utility programs may be used.

LOGOwriter and BASIC Graphics entries will be judged on:

- Your ability to use the features in the LOGOwriter program
- Originality and creativity
- Artistic presentation on the computer screen
- How much you are involved in using the computer

Educational Games (Grades 6–12):

1. No commercial games may be used in conjunction with the contestant's program.
2. The program for a game that you create must allow the children playing with it to be involved.

Educational Games entries will be judged on:

- Sophistication of the program
- Freedom from errors
- Use of color and animation
- Creativity and originality

Submit your entry to your school in March. If you are a student in Grades 3–12 you can submit an entry in more than one category. For example, if you are in Grades 3–5 you can enter both the Story Writing and LOGOwriter Graphics categories. In each contest category the judges will choose three finalists. If you are chosen as one of these finalists at the school level, you will compete in the area contest. In April the judges will choose four top finalists in each category who will compete in the citywide contest. Citywide winners are announced in April. In May there is a Computer Contest Awards Ceremony.

An example of a winning entry in the LOGOwriter Graphics category a few years ago was a program that was a drawing of the Boston skyline. Some of the buildings in the skyline were labeled. The winning program asked you to press a certain key on the computer if you wanted to watch the windows in the John Hancock Tower fall out. You could press a different key to watch it snow.

PRIZES FOR 1989 WERE:

Grand Prize: Computer
First Prize: Savings bond
Second and Third prizes: Trophies
Honorable Mention: Trophy
Principal and teacher at winners' schools in each category: Plaques

What do you think we should tell other kids about the contest you won?

. . . .

"Lots of people always say they would never win so why do it (I said this, too), but I did and won. So I would probably say to them to go for it!"

Ted Iszler

How did you feel when you won?

. . . .

"I wanted to tell everybody in my class. I was proud to win the grand prize in a contest that so many other kids had entered."

Nicholas Saeger

All-American Soap Box Derby

P.O. Box 7233
Derby Downs
Akron, OH 44306

WHO CAN ENTER?

Soap Box Derby racing is open to all kids who qualify and do not exceed the age limit in their division on or before August 1 of each year. You can qualify for the All-American Soap Box Derby in Akron, Ohio, by first competing at the local race level in your hometown. You can also qualify to race at Derby Downs through the Family Rally Program. Guidelines about qualifying are available from the All-American Soap Box Derby headquarters.

There are two racing divisions:
Kit Car Division: Ages 9–16
Masters Division: Ages 11–16

TIME OF YEAR:

August

WHAT IS IT?

For a Soap Box Derby, kids build cars based on rules set up by the All-American Soap Box Derby. In Derby contests, cars must start by gravity from a standstill at a starting line at the top of a hill. No push is allowed. The car whose nose is over the finish line first is the winner.

Boys and girls have built and raced Soap Box Derby cars for decades. The sport has lasted so long because it is fun for families as well as for kids who participate. Beyond that, Soap Box Derby racing is a community affair. Long before you take your car to a race, there are people in the community working together planning the local events. As the future racer, you will get help building your Derby car from an adult or maybe several adults. Every step of the way to your first local race, you will get all the help and encouragement you need.

The Soap Box Derby program is a parent-child program. A parent or other adult is expected to help in the construction of the car. The adult must not build the car but can help by giving advice and being there if needed. There are many rules about what an adult can and cannot do to help you. Be sure you understand and observe all of them.

On race day at the local level, you will match your building skill and driving ability against your competition. If you win, you travel to Akron, Ohio, to race in the All-American Soap Box Derby.

Imagine yourself arriving at the Derby. As a winner from your local competition, you'll be whisked to the welcoming ceremonies in downtown Akron by a police escort with sirens wailing. The Derby band strikes up. You are soon introduced to a crowd of thousands. After signing in on the official entry board, you leave for Derbytown, which is a YMCA camp near Akron. This camp is your home for Derby week. You will make friends with other local Derby winners and have a chance to relax, swim, ride horses, and participate in other sports. Sound like fun?

As Derby week progresses, your car will be weighed and inspected to make sure it meets the standards in the regulations. You get to see Derby Downs, which is a 954-foot racing track, and you get a trial run down the course.

Race day activities begin with a grand track parade, followed by the Oil Can Trophy Race in which TV celebrities compete in bigger Derby cars. Then, at last, the final races are run.

When the race is over and the victories are official, the winners in the Kit Car and Masters divisions get to wear the traditional gold jackets. Awards are presented on Saturday evening. The champions, their families and friends, Derby officials, and business and civic leaders gather at an Akron theatre to pay tribute to all the contestants. All contestants in the All-American are considered winners. They won't soon forget working and having fun together at the Derby.

Even if you aren't into making a Derby car, you might want to go to Akron. Some groups of kids and adults go together by bus to enjoy the race and cheer on their local winner.

The materials needed to build a car are available in kit form from the All-American Soap Box Derby, Inc. in Akron, Ohio. You will need to contact the organization for details about how to order them and to find out who your regional director is. You may obtain the rules by writing to Derby headquarters.

Perhaps you can help turn this event into a community affair. Try to convince your local Derby Director or special Derby committee to plan some great parties during the weekend of local racing.

PRIZES:

Kit Car Division

First Place: Derby watch, trophy, racing clothes, gifts, a $2,500 scholarship, and a trip to Disney World
Second Place: Trophy and $1,500 scholarship
Third Place: Trophy and $1,000 scholarship
Fourth–Ninth places: Trophies

Outstanding Achievement Recognition for best construction (wood car), for originality in decoration, and for best Jetstar construction. (Jetstar is a kind of body you can purchase.)

Masters Division

First Place: Derby watch, trophy, $5,000 scholarship, car tires, and a trip to Disney World
Second Place: Trophy, clock, and $3,000 scholarship
Third Place: Trophy, clock, and $2,000 scholarship
Fourth–Ninth places: Trophies

Outstanding Achievement Recognition for best construction (non-shell), for originality in design (lay down), for originality in design (lean forward), for originality in decoration, and for best speedster construction.

What do you think we should tell other kids about the contest you won?
....

"Get plenty of practice. Don't worry about how you do, just have a lot of fun."

Tami Jo Sullivan

National Model Airplane Championships

Academy of Model Aeronautics (AMA)
1810 Samuel Morse Drive
Reston, VA 22090

WHO CAN ENTER?
Ages up to 14. You must be a member of AMA.

TIME OF YEAR:
End of July

WHAT IS IT?
Competitors fly miniature aircraft in 70 different events in four categories: indoor flight, free flight, control line flight, and radio control flight. Indoor planes are powered by rubber bands; outdoor planes are powered by single-cylinder engines.

Did you ever make a paper airplane in school and aim it at your best friend when the teacher's back was turned? And where did it go? Right over the teacher's head. Whoosh! Uh-oh!

Well, by now you probably know all airplanes have to be controlled in order to land where they are supposed to. Would you like to build a miniature plane and fly it? The Academy of Model Aeronautics can answer all your questions and help you get started. With their guidance, the hobby and sport of aeromodeling is made safe and fun. Local and regional competitions are sponsored by almost all of the more than 1,900 AMA chartered clubs, and winners from the regionals attend the National Model Airplane Championships.

When you fly your model in competition it will be judged on realism, duration of flight, distance, speed, and altitude of flight. All these things will be counted in your score. Sometimes model planes are flown together, as in racing events. Other model planes are judged individually for their aerobatic maneuvers. Miniature planes are made from materials ranging from lightweight wood (balsa) to space-age plastics. Despite many new plastics, balsa remains the favorite construction material of the model builder because it is strong, light, and easy to use.

PRIZES:
Trophies and merchandise prizes from manufacturers

SEAFAIR U.S. West Communications Milk Carton Derby

SEAFAIR
The Westin Building, Suite 2800
2001 Sixth Avenue
Seattle, WA 98121-2574

WHO CAN ENTER?

Children age eight and under must be accompanied by an adult. Individuals or groups can enter in the following categories and age groups:

Racing: Ages 8–13, 14–adult
Open: Ages 8–13, 14–adult
Commercial: For companies
Military: For military personnel
Showboat: Open to everyone
Design competition: Awards will be given for the best design

TIME OF YEAR:

July

WHAT IS IT?

All-day, free, fun event rewarding creativity and teamwork. This contest involves everyone in the design, creation, and building of boats and other floating vessels from milk cartons.

Children design and put together milk cartons and make a boat. The boat must float. To enter, drink lots of milk and waterproof your cartons. Use your imagination...almost anything will float. Past entries have been a Statue of Liberty, a banana, and a giant treadmill. Make your plans and use waterproof glue.

You'll need to estimate the number of milk cartons you'll use. These boats and vessels have to support you as you compete in the races. It takes twenty-five half-gallon cartons to float a hundred pounds. One quart will float two pounds, and a half gallon will float four.

Decide what will power your boat—feet, fins, arms, or paddles. All entries can be in the Parade of Boats. For more information and rules and regulations for building your milk-carton float, write to the address above. U.S. West Communications will give ten cents for every milk carton used in the Derby to an area youth organization.

The Derby is divided into the following classifications:

Racing: Includes all vessels designed for speed

Open: Any entry that is not included in the other categories

Commercial: This category is for companies, event sponsors, and SEAFAIR families. A trophy will be awarded to the winner of the commercial race.

Showboat: For entries who wish to take part in the Parade of Boats

PRIZES:

Grand Showboat Award: Four round-trip tickets to anywhere in the United States that Continental Airlines flies

There are over $5,000 in prizes for winners in other categories

WHAT ARE MY CHANCES?

Last year there were 92 entrants and 14 won prizes.

United States Model Rocket Championships

National Association of Rocketry
182 Madison Drive
Elizabeth, PA 15037

WHO CAN ENTER?

Division A: Ages up to 14
Division B: Ages 15–17
Division C: Ages 18 and over

TIME OF YEAR:

August

WHAT IS IT?

People of all ages who have built model rockets show them and launch them in competition.

You've built your model of the Saturn rocket from a great kit. It was long, hard work. Maybe you're interested in entering your model in a contest. Or perhaps you want to learn how to launch it into flight so that you can compete in height and distance events. For that, you'll need help from a hobby store owner, members of your local model rocket club, or from another adult experienced in model rocket flight. You'll learn the basics of launching and either borrow or purchase a launch pad, an ignition system, and an ignition battery. Now you're ready to launch your rocket.

Today, model rockets range from simple, low-cost, easy-to-build kits to complex scale models built from scratch that represent hundreds of hours of work. Model rocket engines, safety-certified by the National Association of Rocketry and made only by professional manufacturers, are available in most hobby stores. A common-sense safety code ensures that model rocketry is safe.

In model rocket competitions there are over two dozen types of events. These include scale model competitions, rocket glider events, flight duration categories, plastic model flights, high-powered altitude trials, and radio control events. You can even compete in "egg lofting," an event you win by lofting an egg to the highest altitude and recovering it unbroken. At the United States

Model Rocket Championships, you'll compete against other kids your age in events such as altitude flights, parachute duration, streamer duration, scale models, and research and development of rocket models. Generally there are 10 events flown each year at the Championships.

PRIZES:

Trophies are awarded in each age division.

All events are covered in the National Association of Rocketry's monthly magazine, *American Spacemodeling*.

How did you feel when you won?

. . . .

"I felt like I really accomplished something."

Brandon Bauman

Annual Poetry Contest for Students

Walt Whitman House
246 Old Walt Whitman Road
Huntington Station, NY 11746

WHO CAN ENTER?

Open to students in Grades 3 through 12 who currently live on Long
Island, New York

Entrance categories:

A: Individual poems written by pupils, Grades 3–4

B: Individual poems written by pupils, Grades 5–6

C: Individual poems written by pupils, Grades 7–8

D: Class anthology of poems, Grades 3–6

E: Class anthology of poems, Grades 7–8

F: Individual poems written by pupils, Grades 9–10

G: Class anthology of poems, Grades 9–10

H: Individual poems written by pupils, Grades 11–12

I: Class anthology of poems, Grades 11–12

TIME OF YEAR:

Entries accepted January 15 through March 31

WHAT IS IT?

Children write poems about Long Island in the style of Walt Whitman,
Long Island's greatest poet.

The theme of the contest varies from year to year. Children are
often encouraged to write catalogue poems in which they list the
things they have seen, for example, on a class trip to a natural area.
Poets should include as many specific details as possible, such as
names of birds and trees, or specific feelings. Write to the Walt
Whitman House for the theme of the year.

The rules of the contest are:

1. All entries must be typewritten, computer typed, or printed in ink using double spacing on a standard 8½" × 11" paper, and be clearly legible.
2. All entries must be no longer than two typewritten pages.
3. Individual poems should be headed with the following information on each page:
   - Entrance category
   - Entrant's name, address, age, and grade level
   - Entrant's school and teacher's name
4. Class anthology entries should be securely bound together and include the following information:
   - A title page with the school name and address, teacher's name, grade level, and entrance category
   - Each individual poem should be titled with the child's name
5. Anthologies will be returned if accompanied by a self-addressed, stamped envelope.
6. Individual entries will NOT be returned.

The Birthplace Association and Marine Midland Bank reserve the right to reject any entry that does not conform to the aforementioned standards of format.

PRIZES:

First Place individual winner: Will be published in "Starting from Paumanok"

First, Second, and Honorable Mention awards: Will be given to entries from each category

BOOK IT!® National Reading Incentive Program

Pizza Hut®, Inc.
P.O. Box 2999
Wichita, KS 67201

WHO CAN ENTER?

Students in Grades K–6 whose teachers decide to run a BOOK IT!® program

TIME OF YEAR:

October 1–February 28 annually

WHAT IS IT?

For the BOOK IT!® program, teachers decide on the number of pages or number of books that each participant in the class must read in a month. When kids have finished the amount required, they are awarded a Free Pizza Award Certificate good for a Personal Pan Pizza® at any participating Pizza Hut® restaurant.

Maybe you like to read but nobody seems to notice how many books you read on your own. Or maybe you don't like to read and everybody notices and tries to urge you to read more. Either way, whether you like to read or you don't, we bet you like to eat pizza. Hmm? Well, how would you like to read, fast or slow, and get to eat pizza as a reward? You would? The BOOK IT!® program run by Pizza Hut® makes it possible for you to do just that.

Here's how the program works. First of all, you have to get your teachers and principal interested in running the program. Before June every year, they have to send for the materials to help them set up the BOOK IT!® program at your school for the following year. Then once your school is enrolled, your teacher's job is to set up a reading contract with you, with your class, or even set up a way all kids in the school can participate. The teacher decides on a minimum number of books or a minimum number of pages each child is to read per month.

When you have reached the month's goal, you will get a Free Pizza Award Certificate, good for one Personal Pan Pizza® at any participating Pizza Hut®. If you read more than the required amount in any month, good for you! Your teacher and your parents will be proud of you. But you can't be awarded more than one certificate for any one month. Sorry!

But there's another kind of prize to work for in the BOOK IT!® program. If all the kids in your class read the minimum amount and get certificates in four out of five months, your class will win a free pizza party from Pizza Hut®. (Sorry, kindergarteners aren't eligible for the party.) You can have the pizza party as an outdoor picnic. Or your class can sit at a table of honor in the school lunchroom for the party. Besides that, you and your classmates can invite a local personality to attend your party. This might mean a special news feature about your class in your town paper. Then everyone will see your picture and know what a good reader you are becoming.

PRIZES:

Level 1 (student reads a minimum amount within a calendar month): Pizza Award Certificate for one Personal Pan Pizza®

Level 2 (student reads the minimum amount in all five months of the program): Reader's Honor Roll

Level 3 (each student in a class achieves the minimum monthly goal in any four of the five months): Free pizza party for the class (except kindergartens)

Can you tell us how you got started in the activity?
. . . .

"The reading teacher told us and I chose a book that I wanted to read."

Nikisha Small

How did you feel when you won?
. . . .

"Excited and I didn't think I had heard correctly (unbelievable)."

Kellie O'Shields

INVENT AMERICA! Contest

United States Patent Model Foundation
510 King Street, Suite 420
Alexandria, VA 22314

WHO CAN ENTER?

Open to all children in Kindergarten–Grade 8

TIME OF YEAR:

Early May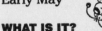

WHAT IS IT?

Kids create inventions using their imagination and creativity.

Did you ever think how much fun it would be to take one of your ideas and turn it into a great invention? If you never thought about being an inventor before, you'll be surprised to find out how many great inventions are just simple solutions to everyday problems. Even ideas that seem wild or crazy are sometimes the best. That's why the theme of the contest is "Let your imagination fly."

Once you dream up an idea for an invention, you'll need to test it to make sure the concept really works. This is the challenging part, because sometimes you'll have to redesign or improve on your idea as you go along. The effort is worth it, though, because when you're done, you can enter your invention in the national INVENT AMERICA! contest.

Most kids enter this contest through their classrooms at school or through after-school clubs or programs. Many kids keep an inventor's log on their progress and learn about our country's patent system as part of their invention project.

To enter the INVENT AMERICA! contest, you must fill out an official entry form to describe your invention and make an illustration of your idea. If you're in Kindergarten or Grades 1–3, your teacher or parent can help you fill out the entry form, but the content and illustration must be your own work.

Then you turn in your entry form to your teacher. Kids compete based on grade level. If your idea is picked as a grade-level winner for your state, you'll get a prize and a chance to go on and compete at the regional level. There are five regions and nine winners from each region, one for each grade level. If the judges pick your idea to represent your grade at the regional level, you'll get another award, you and your parents and teacher will get a free trip to Washington, D.C. to take part in the National INVENT AMERICA! Week. There you will compete for one of the nine national awards.

Last year the national winners were selected by a panel of 19 distinguished judges, which included U.S. senators and congresspeople, corporate executives, famous inventors, authors, patent attorneys, and publishers. President George Bush sent a special commendation to the awards ceremony. The national winners' inventions were also displayed at the Smithsonian Institution! State, regional, and national winners got their names and pictures in more than 2,000 magazines and newspapers across the country, and some winners even appeared on television.

PRIZES:

In 1991, prizes included U.S. savings bonds of up to $1,000 for kids and prizes for winners' teachers and schools, including books, computers, flags, and banners. Brad Bolerjack and Katherine Szudy went to Japan to receive international honors for their inventions.

What did you like best about this contest?

. . . .

"Best of all I liked the trip my family took to Washington, D.C. because the judges liked my idea. It gave me a chance to learn a lot about our country and to meet many wonderful people."

Lisa Ann Labadie

MADD (Mothers Against Drunk Driving) Essay Contest

MADD National Youth Programs
P.O. Box 541688
Dallas, TX 75354-1688

WHO CAN ENTER?

Grades 4–6
Grades 7–9
Grades 10–12

TIME OF YEAR:

Local contests: Time varies
Individual Entry and National Contest Judging: March

WHAT IS IT?

An essay contest about the dangers of drinking and driving.

Drunk driving is a very serious problem in the United States. In fact, accidents involving drinking are one of the leading causes of death for young people. The MADD essay contest challenges you to write about a theme on the dangers of drunk driving. You have up to 250 words, typed or neatly printed, on one page to encourage people to avoid drinking and driving. Make sure you also include the official entry form with your essay.

Explain why drunk driving is so dangerous and make sure that you encourage people to stay far away from it. It's for a good cause, so try your best to be persuasive. Help teach people about the dangers of drinking and driving. Good luck!

PRIZES:

Local contests
Prizes decided upon locally

National "Individual Entry" contest
First Prize: $100 and plaque
Second Prize: $50 and plaque
Third Prize: $25 and plaque

National contests

First Prize for each grade division: $1,000, trophy, and all-expense-paid trip to New York City with a chaperone for an awards ceremony sponsored by the National Highway Traffic Safety Administration

Second Prize for each grade division: $500 and plaque

Third Prize for each grade division: $250 and plaque

Mathematical Olympiads for Elementary Schools

Dr. George Lenchner
125 Merle Avenue
Oceanside, NY 11572

WHO CAN ENTER?

Grades K–6

TIME OF YEAR:

Five Olympiads are held about one month apart, usually beginning in November and continuing through March.

WHAT IS IT?

School teams complete special problems proposed by the Mathematical Olympiads organization. Individuals and teams are eligible for awards.

Do you and your friends like to solve math problems? Are you and your teachers looking for fun ways to increase your skills at problem solving? Over 75,000 kids in 3,000 schools from New York to New Zealand and the Azores to the United Arab Emirates participate in the Mathematical Olympiads for Elementary Schools. You and your school team can participate, too, by getting a teacher to help you start a team. And, if there are more than 35 kids who want to join in the fun, your school can have several teams.

Each year, packets are sent to participating schools in November, December, January, February, and March. The Olympiad packets contain copies of the Olympiad problems, an answers and solutions sheet, a score sheet, directions for administering the Olympiad, and an envelope for returning the completed score sheet. On a designated day, kids work to solve the problems. Sometimes the school chooses to give all the problems at once, and sometimes there are small rests between problems, but there is always a time limit for each problem. For example, here is a problem given in December 1985 with a 4-minute time limit:

Tom multiplied a number by 2½ and got 50 as an answer. However, he should have divided the number by 2½ to get the correct answer. What is the correct answer?

Here's another problem to be done in 5 minutes:

Carol bought apples at 3 for 25¢ but sold them at 2 for 25¢. One day she made a profit of $1. How many apples did she sell on that day?

Once your team has completed the problems for the five Olympiads, your score sheet can be sent to the Mathematical Olympiad office and you may be eligible for many awards.

PRIZES:

Each participating student: Certificate

Students with cumulative scores exceeding a designated limit: Embroidered Olympiad patch

Highest individual scorer on each team: Trophy

Students in the top 10% of the individual scoring: Silver or gold Olympiad Pin

Each student with a perfect score: Olympiad Medallion

Each school with outstanding team score: Plaque

Each school with high team score: Certificate

What did you like best about the contest?

....

"The thing I liked best about this contest was that it gave me a chance to think things through and sort them out. When the contest was over, my math skills had improved, and I had learned techniques for solving problems."

Karen Galvin

Morgan Horse Essay and Poem Contest

Department of Youth and Education
American Morgan Horse Association
P.O. Box 960
Shelburne, VT 05482

WHO CAN ENTER?

Anyone under the age of 21

TIME OF YEAR:

December

WHAT IS IT?

Kids write essays or poems on a theme set by the American Morgan Horse Association.

If you love horses, this contest might be for you. If you also like to write poetry or essays, then it is definitely for you! Find out as much as you can about Morgan horses. Then use your creativity and imagination to write an essay or poem about Morgan horses.

Essays must be 1,000 words or less and must be based on the special theme set by the AMHA. The theme in 1991 was "My Morgan Horse: A Super Hero." Essays and poems will be judged on originality, general style, grammar, and punctuation.

Write to the AMHA to find out this year's theme and for more details.

PRIZES:

First Place: $25.00
Second, Third, Fourth, and Fifth places: Ribbons

Morgan Horse Show Youth Bowl Contest

Department of Youth and Education
American Morgan Horse Association
P.O. Box 960
Shelburne, VT 05482

WHO CAN ENTER?

Teams from the American Morgan Horse Association, 4-H, Future Farmers of America, Pony Club, or other breed-affiliated clubs

TIME OF YEAR:

October

WHAT IS IT?

Teams from horse clubs compete in question-and-answer matches.

For this contest, put together a team of four people from the club you belong to. Study hard to learn all you can about horses and horse competitions. Then enter the Morgan Horse Youth Bowl Contest and test your knowledge.

The questions in this competition are taken from the following books:

1. *The Morgan Horse* by Jeanne Mellin Herrick
2. *The Morgan Horse Handbook* by Jeanne Mellin Herrick
3. *The Complete Morgan Horse* by Jeanne Mellin Herrick
4. *The Morgan Horse Judging Standards Manual*
5. *The AMHA Registration Rules Booklet*
6. *The AMHAY Horsemastership Program*
7. *The AHSA Rule Book*
8. *Lameness in the Horse* by O. R. Adams, DVM
9. *Horses* by J. W. Evans
10. *The Illustrated Veterinary Encyclopedia for Horsemen*
11. *Equus Magazine* (current year, starting with the January issue)
12. *Feeding and Care of the Horse* by Lon Lewis

Two teams compete against one another at a time. A question is asked, and the first team to answer it correctly scores a point. For every correct answer a point is added; for every wrong answer a point is subtracted. At the end of the match the team with the higher score will go on to compete against another team. At the end of the contest the 10 highest scoring teams receive prizes. The highest individual scores are also awarded.

PRIZES:

Ten Highest Scoring Teams and Individuals: Plaques, ribbons, horse models, notecards, and books

National Bicentennial Competition on the Constitution and Bill of Rights

Center for Civic Education
5146 Douglas Fir Road
Calabasas, CA 91302

WHO CAN ENTER?

All schoolchildren in the United States

TIME OF YEAR:

All year

WHAT IS IT?

The Commission on the Bicentennial of the United States Constitution and the Center for Civic Education sponsors competitions about the Constitution. The competitions are held in schools throughout the United States.

Do you know what "Bicentennial of the Constitution" is? It means that it's been 200 years since the Constitution was written. These competitions are designed to make you and the rest of the kids in the United States more aware of how the Constitution was planned and adopted by the people of our nation 200 years ago.

In 1987 the National Bicentennial Competition was started for high school students. In 1988 the program was made available to elementary and junior high school students. The programs will be organized on the local level by Congressional district—so the help and interest of teachers, community leaders, elected officials, parents, and students is important for the program to be a success. Watch for updates on the program.

The program has two parts:

Instructional Program: Your school will receive a specially prepared instruction unit about the Constitution. This unit helps teach:

- The basic ideas behind our Constitution
- The history that led to the writing of the Constitution
- What the Constitution says
- How the Constitution established our government
- The rights and responsibilities the Constitution gives to citizens

Competitive Program: Classes that choose to participate in the competitive portion of the program work together as a team to demonstrate knowledge of the Constitution. There are written and oral tests.

PRIZES:

Awards are presented by members of Congress and other prominent officials.

FOR MORE INFORMATION:

Write to your local member of Congress or to the address above.

How did you find out about the contest?

....

"I found out about it one day someone quit and the people that were already in the group asked me if I would fill that position. So I said sure but I really didn't know what I was getting into at first."

Tobey Reynolds

National History Day

11201 Euclid Avenue
Cleveland, OH 44106

WHO CAN ENTER?

Grades 6–12

TIME OF YEAR:

Spring

WHAT IS IT?

The National History Day competition encourages students to conduct extensive research on a topic related to an annual theme. Contestants can present their research in one of seven categories:
- Historical Papers
- Individual Projects
- Group Projects
- Individual Dramatic Performances
- Group Dramatic Performances
- Individual Media Presentations
- Group Media Presentations

Contestants should choose a category in which they can best use their talents and abilities.

Here are the contest rules:

1. Historical Papers: Papers must be no less than 1,500 and no more than 2,500 words long. Footnotes are required. The papers must be typed. Four copies of a paper must be submitted with the appropriate entry form.
2. Projects: The overall size of the project must be no larger than 40 inches wide, 30 inches long, and 6 feet high. The media devices used in the project cannot run for more than 3 minutes. The written materials used on the project cannot be more than 500 words. Students cannot give a prepared introduction to the project.
3. Performances: Performances must be no longer than 10 minutes. Use of slides, tape recorders, and computers is permitted. The title of the entry must be announced at the beginning of the performance.

Student entries are judged by professional historians and educators. Many competitions are held on college and university campuses.

PRIZES:

State and District Contest Prizes

Books, cash awards, and plaques

National Prizes

First Prize: $1,000

Second Prize: $500

Third Prize: $200

Special Prizes: Vary from year to year; include a full-tuition, four-year scholarship to Western Reserve University

WHAT ARE MY CHANCES?

Last year there were over 400,000 entries nationwide and over 1,700 entries to the national events. Prizes were awarded in 14 categories at each level of competition (district, state, and national).

Odyssey of the Mind (OM) Competitions

Odyssey of the Mind Association, Inc.
P.O. Box 27
Glassboro, NJ 08028

WHO CAN ENTER?

Division I: Kindergarten–Grade 5
Division II: Grades 6–8
Division III: Grades 9–12
Division IV: Collegiate

TIME OF YEAR:

World Finals usually in May or early June; problems given to teams in the fall

WHAT IS IT?

Teams work on problems and find creative solutions.

To most people, a mousetrap is for catching mice. But to kids engaged in an OM competition several years ago, a mousetrap had other uses. It was used to turn the wheels of a vehicle called a "mousemobile." The mousemobile was used in competition against other groups of kids. Wonder what the mice in the building thought about it?

Each year, the OM competitions challenge students to find creative answers to several tough problems. A team has from fall to the time of competition to come up with a solution to the problems assigned. Divisions I and III are eligible to compete in four problems; Division II is eligible for five problems. The teams that win the local and regional competitions are allowed to enter the World Finals. At the 1990 Finals, over 600 teams participated, and 11,000 people attended. There are 53 sanctioned OM associations—in 45 states, Washington, D.C., British Columbia, Alberta, Ontario, and as far away as China and the U.S.S.R.

A team effort is probably the strongest principle in the OM competitions. When the judges look at a team's work, they are looking for unusual ideas and for style of presentation. In the case of the mousemobile relays, the kids who reached the finals worked for up to six months on their solution and then won local and regional competitions before going on to the World Finals.

In OM competitions, teams are judged in three areas. The first is the long-term problem, that is, the solution on which the team has been working prior to competition and that they bring to the event. The second area is the style competition. Art, music, drama, and costume design are used to make the solutions more outstanding and unique. For example, one mousemobile team made costumes and prepared a skit about mice. They marched into the competition in their costumes, presented their skit, and raced their mousemobiles for the style competition. The third area is a spontaneous problem. This is a problem that is given to the team on the day of competition. The team must solve it on the spot without any preparation. For example, they might be asked to think of as many "keys" as they can. Teams receive one point for answers like "car keys" or "safe-deposit-box keys." They earn three points for imaginative answers, such as "monkey."

OM competitions turn out to be lots of fun because kids have to be creative and able to cooperate with other people to win. Some problems that teams have solved are:

- Designing and constructing a vehicle that will fit into two suitcases
- Using mousetraps to trigger a chain reaction
- Constructing a balsa-wood structure that ranges in height from 8 to 8½ inches (the more weight the structure holds, the more points awarded)
- Creating and giving a presentation that takes place in a cave in prehistoric times
- Creating and presenting a tea party, complete with props and dress

OM competitions are usually coached by an adult such as a teacher, group leader, or the parent of a team member.

PRIZES:

World Finals

First Prize: Gold medals for each team member and a trophy for their school

Second Prize: Silver medals for each team member and a trophy for their school

Third Prize: Bronze medals for each team member and a trophy for their school

The Ranatra Fusca Creativity Award

Awarded to the individual or group showing outstanding creative problem-solving skills. Why is the award called by this name? Some years ago, a student tried to create a water flotation device that would help him to walk on water, and it looked a lot like a water spider (*Ranatra fusca*). He did not have enough time to perfect his invention, so he kept falling in the water when he tried to use it. The problems weren't all solved, but the student had shown a lot of imagination. So this award was named after his spiderlike creation.

State and Regional Awards

Trophies, plaques, and ribbons (awards differ from state to state)

WHAT ARE MY CHANCES?

In 1990, 634 teams entered the World Finals competition, and 63 won awards.

P. A. Witty Outstanding Literature Award

Dr. Cathy Collins
Professor
School of Education
P.O. Box 32925
Texas Christian University
Fort Worth, TX 76129

WHO CAN ENTER?

Elementary and secondary school students

TIME OF YEAR:

Entries should be sent by February 1, 1992. Final decisions will be made by May 15.

WHAT IS IT?

Kids can send original poems, stories, or prose to this writing award contest sponsored by the International Reading Association. Writing is judged on its creativity, originality, and beauty of expression.

Here are the rules:
1. Elementary school students' entries must be legible and not longer than 1,000 words. Secondary school students' entries should be typed and may be longer than 1,000 words if necessary.
2. If poetry is entered, a set of five poems must be submitted.
3. All entries and requests for applications must include a self-addressed, stamped envelope.
4. Teachers who submit students' writing should be certain that the work is creative and personally done by the student. The teachers of those students selected will be notified.

PRIZES:
$25 and a certificate of merit

Rocky Mountain Philatelic Exhibition

Rocky Mountain Philatelic Exhibitions, Inc. (ROMPEX)
P.O. Box 2352
Denver, CO 80201

WHO CAN ENTER?

Anyone under age 18 enters the Juniors section, Section 7.

TIME OF YEAR:

April

WHAT IS IT?

Kids who have stamp collections prepare a portfolio of their collection to show in the exhibition.

Many kids we know have stamp collections, and maybe you do, too! You can organize your stamps in a loose-leaf notebook, or, if you decide to get really fancy, you can put them in plastic covers to protect them from dust, dirt, and spills. By organizing your stamps in a notebook you'll be able to admire all the stamps you've collected and show them off to your parents and friends. To add new stamps to your collection, check with the post office in your town to see what kinds of stamps they have in stock. Once you build up your collection, you may even want to show them off in an exhibition put on by you and your stamp-collecting friends.

To enter the Rocky Mountain Philatelic Exhibition, send a description of your exhibit on the official entry form. Your parents or guardian must also sign your entry form. All entry forms must be received by April 1 of the current year. There is a limit on the number of entries the Exhibits Committee will accept, so be sure to submit your entry form early. You may enter more than one exhibit, but you must fill out a separate entry form for each exhibit you enter. There is no entry fee for junior exhibits.

Junior exhibits are limited to a maximum of 6 frames per exhibit (there are 16 pages in a frame).

If your entry is accepted by the Exhibits Committee, you send in your exhibit to the committee by the May 1 deadline. If you are a winner of the ROMPEX Grand Award, you will be eligible to participate in the American Philatelic Society (APS) Champion of Champions competition. The exhibits will be judged in open competition by a panel of APS-accredited judges.

PRIZES:

First Place: ROMPEX Gold Medal
Second Place: Vermeil Medal
Third Place: Silver Medal
Fourth Place: Silver-Bronze Medal
Fifth Place: Bronze Medal
All Exhibitors: Certificates of Participation

California State Elementary Spelling Championship

c/o Sonoma County Office of Education
Room 111E
410 Fiscal Drive
Santa Rosa, CA 95403

WHO CAN ENTER?
Any student in Grades 4–6 in the state of California

TIME OF YEAR:
May

WHAT IS IT?
Kids who win spelling bees in their classrooms, their schools, their regions, and then their counties are eligible for the California State Elementary Spelling Championship. Sample words are supplied by the Sonoma County Office of Education.

If you live in California and you've gotten through all three competitions up to the state level, you'll have a great time on California State Elementary Spelling Championship day. When you arrive, you'll be given a badge with a ribbon and your number for the spelling competition. You'll sit in the seat with that number and be called by that number for your turn to spell. When you're called, you'll walk up to the podium to spell out your round. The first time you miss a word—oops!—you'll be eliminated. The last three rounds are the ones in which the spellers spell against each other, just like in the Scripps Howard bees. (See next contest.)

When the competition is over, there will be a luncheon at which you can get to meet kids from all over the state. There will also be a speaker, and the awards will be handed out to the six winners.

PRIZES:
Trophies and savings bonds

Scripps Howard National Spelling Bee

1100 Central Trust Tower
Cincinnati, OH 45202

WHO CAN ENTER?

Contestants must not have passed beyond 8th grade in school nor be older than 16 years at the time of the National Finals.

TIME OF YEAR:

School Championships: March
Regional Finals: April
National Finals: May

WHAT IS IT?

Kids who win spelling bees in their classrooms, schools, counties, and states are eligible for the National Spelling Bee.

The kids are sitting on the edges of their seats in the school auditorium. The only contestants left in your school's spelling bee are you and Sam Jones, an 8th grader. The word pronouncer gives Sam his next word, "condominium." Sam spells slowly, "con-do-mi-i-um." He spelled it wrong! Now it's your turn. You spell, loudly, "con-do-min-i-um," and you're right! Now you have to spell one more word, "chrysanthemum," which you spell correctly, and you're the school champion! The kids clap like crazy—some even whistle— and you hear, "Way to go!" Now you're going to go to the regional finals, and maybe you'll win those. Then you'll get a free trip to Washington, D.C. to the National Spelling Bee.

Every year, kids in the 4th through 8th grades participate in school spelling bees sponsored by their local newspapers. The school holds a bee using spelling words provided by the Scripps Howard National Spelling Bee and following rules for competition supplied by the newspapers. Kids start with contests in their class-rooms, learning how to listen to the words and to spell out loud correctly. Teachers usually distribute a book, *Words of Champions,* that is available from Scripps Howard. The book contains practice spelling words that will be used in the contests, and kids can work on spelling both at school and at home. The 1991 edition of the book costs 29¢.

In the contests, kids usually stand in a group, and the teacher acts as the "pronouncer." The kids learn that all contestants have a chance to spell a word as their turn comes up. Upon missing the spelling of a word, a contestant immediately drops out of the contest. The next word on the pronouncer's list is given to the next contestant. When the contestants are reduced to two, the elimination procedure changes. At that point, when one contestant misspells a word, the other contestant is given an opportunity to spell that same word. If the second contestant spells that word correctly, plus the next word on the pronouncer's list, then the second contestant shall be declared the champion. Sometimes school and regional contests are run with kids writing out their answers, but at the National Spelling Bee the competition is always done orally.

PRIZES:

National Finals

In 1989, 222 winners shared over $16,000 worth of prizes at the Nationals in Washington, D.C.

Regional Championships

First Prize: All-expenses-paid trip accompanied by one adult, to the National Spelling Bee in Washington, D.C., and a set of *Encyclopedia Britannica*

Other winners: Computers, color TV sets, *Webster's Dictionaries* and *Random House Dictionaries,* typewriters, and gift certificates at local malls

School Competitions

First, Second, and Third Prize winners: Medals and certificates

United States National Elementary Chess Championship

Scholastic Coordinator
U.S. Chess Federation (USCF)
186 Route 9W
New Windsor, NY 12550

WHO CAN ENTER?

Students in Grades 1–6 who know how to play chess may enter by filling out a form in the USCF newsletter *School Mates,* or by requesting a special flier on the event from USCF.

TIME OF YEAR:

Nationals: April or early May
Other tournaments: Year-round, but especially during the school months

WHAT IS IT?

Chess tournaments are held at schools, in clubs, and at the state and regional levels. All young players are welcome to play in the National Elementary Championship. For some of the competitions, however, you must be a member of the U.S. Chess Federation or be from the area in which they are held.

Playing chess will give you lots of practice in planning and problem solving. At chess, you win by thinking. It is not like checkers, which you win by taking the most pieces from your opponent. In chess, the idea is to plan your moves so that you can trap your opponent's king. You can play chess on a computer, although it is almost impossible to beat a computer. You can also play chess through the mail. That's right! You can have a chess pal, just like you can have a pen pal. You can also play with another person through a computer. Imagine that!

Would you like to start a chess club at school? Do you need to find out where the nearest chess club is? The United States Chess

Federation can help you do both of these things. The USCF can even tell you where some clubs are near you. When you write to the USCF, be sure to give your age, since you can qualify for a youth membership. If you join, you'll get issues of *Chess Life,* and there is also a special magazine just for players ages 12 and under. If your school forms a club, your sponsor can ask to receive *School Mates,* a newsletter that reports on school programs across the nation, tips from school coaches, and the lists of the top 50 best players nationally in six age categories: under 8 years, 9–10, 11–12, 12–14, and over 14. Ask your teacher to help you. There may be financial help available for your school group from the U.S. Chess Trust. Other places to get information about chess are local newspapers, game stores, libraries, and school district offices.

PRIZES:

More than 125 trophies and plaques are awarded to individual players and best teams.

How did you feel when you won?

....

"I was so excited I couldn't speak."

Karen Stewart

Science Olympiad

5955 Little Pine Lane
Rochester, MI 48064

WHO CAN ENTER?
Division A: Grades 3–6
Division B: Grades 6–9
Division C: Grades 9–12

TIME OF YEAR:
May

WHAT IS IT?
Students solve scientific problems, either in teams or individually.

You can learn more about biology, physics, chemistry, computers, and technology by being involved in science experiments that excite you. Maybe you'd like to watch birds as they feed from the bird feeder near your bedroom window. As you observe and write notes, you're doing biology! Or, maybe you like to identify and mix certain chemical substances together. As you write down your observations, you're doing chemistry! If you work with a friend, check to see if your observations are the same or different and try to discover reasons for your findings.

Each year the Science Olympiad Executive Board has approximately 23 events for the Olympiad. Each event falls under one of three goal areas. We list the three goal areas and a few examples of past events in the Science Olympiad for kids 6 to 12. Then we have explained a few events to give you an idea of the kinds of events in the Science Olympiad.

In the Science Concepts and Knowledge area, past projects to be solved were: No Bones About It, Rock Hound, and Science Bowl. In the Science Processes and Thinking Skills areas, past projects included: Large Number Estimation, Map Reading, Mystery Boxes, and Mystery Powders. In the Science Application and Thinking

Skills areas, past projects to be solved included: Circuit Wizardry, Reflection Relay, Rubber-Band Catapult, Can-Can Race, and Structures. With the No Bones About It project, a team of two students matched approximately 15 different kinds of bones with a skeleton on a chart. In the Mystery Powders event, a team of two students had to identify mixtures of white household powders. Events are more difficult at higher grade levels.

In Division A, a team consists of up to 12 students. In Divisions B and C, a team consists of up to 15 students. You begin with local or regional competitions. They take place at Science Olympiad tournaments, where 15 to 21 events are run, or at science field days, where only a few selected events are run.

After winning at local and regional events, teams from these divisions can go to the nationals. At the nationals in May, events are run for three days, during which the teams compete in the events they choose. Travel expenses to local, regional, and national tournaments are the responsibility of the team or individual.

An individual child or team can enter only those events listed by the Science Olympiad Executive Board for their division, but may participate in as many projects as they want within their division. Most events require teamwork and group planning, and each event has its own set of rules. Your teacher will explain the rules, which are very easy to understand and to work with.

You or your team must complete a membership application form 30 days before your regional or state tournament. There is a membership fee for Divisions A, B, and C. This fee entitles the member school to a copy of the *Science Olympiad Coaches and Rules Manual*. In addition, the fee makes teams eligible to participate at the first level of competition in their district, region, or state.

Judging of the competitions is done by college professors, coaches, business and industry workers, parents, and administrators.

PRIZES:

National Awards

First–Third places: Medals

Awards for highest score, Divisions B and C: Championship trophies

Local, state, and regional awards, all divisions: Medals and trophies

Young America Horticulture Contests

National Junior Horticultural Association
c/o Jan Hoffman
411 Pine Street
Freemont, MI 49412-1737

WHO CAN ENTER?

Individuals or groups can enter in the following categories and age groups:

Gardening Contest: Ages 8 and under, 9–11, and 12–14

Environmental Beautification Contest: Ages 8 and under, 9–11, and 12–14

Plant Propagation Contest: Ages 8 and under, 9–11, and 12–14

Experimental Horticulture Contest: Ages 8 and under, 9–11, and 12–14

TIME OF YEAR:

October 15

WHAT IS IT?

A contest in which you experiment with growing plants.

If you enjoy growing and experimenting with plants or like seeing how they can make roadsides or riverbanks beautiful, then maybe the Young America Horticulture Contests are for you. Horticulture is the planting and growing of fruits, vegetables, flowers, nuts, herbs, and ornamental plants. The National Junior Horticultural Association sponsors four different contests every year. The contests are Gardening, Environmental Beautification, Plant Propagation, and Experimental Horticulture. You can enter either one or two of them every year. To enter each contest, you have to write a report after you are done with your project and mail it in with some photos before October 15.

Gardening Contest

For this contest you have to raise several kinds of plants. The number of plants you must grow is different for the various age groups: 6 or more plants for kids 8 or younger; 8 or more plants for kids 9–11; and 10 or more plants for kids 12–14. You can raise fruits, vegetables, decorative plants like flowers, or herbs. Some of the plants can be easy to grow, some hard to grow, and some in between. At the end of the growing season you will have to write up a report.

Environmental Beautification Contest

You or your group might clean up a riverbank or a street or vacant lot. Then you can plant and care for some trees and flowers instead of letting the weeds grow wild. For this contest, you'll also need to write up a report and then send some "before and after" photos of your project.

Plant Propagation Contest

For this contest, you grow new plants from seeds or cuttings, or by layering, grafting, or other methods. You have to decide which methods you want to use, do your project, and write a report. Growing new plants is fun—you can give some of them away, sell some, and keep some.

Experimental Horticulture Contest

The last contest is a little more exotic. You can do an experiment with seeds or cuttings or come up with some new ways to grow plants. It's great to try your own original experiment. In this contest you still have to write a report, but you must also analyze your results and explain what they mean. Remember, if you have questions about any of your horticulture experiments, you can get a book from the library to help you.

You can write to the National Junior Horticultural Association for entry forms and tips about how to get started either by yourself or with a group. The material also explains how to do your project, gives suggestions and advice, tells you how to keep the records needed to write your report, and suggests books to read for additional ideas.

PRIZES:

Pins, ribbons, framed certificates, plaques, gift certificates, trophies, and trips

CHAPTER 4

Playing Street, Yard, and Beach Games

American Double Dutch League Competitions

P.O. Box 776
Bronx, NY 10451

WHO CAN ENTER?

Ages 8 and over

TIME OF YEAR:

Usually in warm weather, but check with the American Double Dutch League

WHAT IS IT?

Double Dutch is a jump rope activity in which two ropes are turned simultaneously in eggbeater style by two turners, while a third person jumps within the moving ropes.

The sport of Double Dutch was founded by detective David Walker in 1973, when the New York City Police Community Affairs division was looking for a sports activity specifically designed for young girls. In 1974, Walker and New York City detective Mike Williams founded the American Double Dutch League, the sport's official governing body.

Competitive Double Dutch includes using official American Double Dutch League–approved rules, regulations, and equipment. Teams compete in two divisions—either singles or doubles. Singles teams are made up of two turners and one jumper. Doubles teams are made up of two turners and two jumpers. Some kids think that jumping doubles is the most fun. Then they can do lots of tricks and jump to rhymes and music. In competition, all teams must perform three tests: the speed test, the compulsory tricks test, and the freestyle test. There is an annual American Double Dutch League show, and the best competing teams are invited by the League to compete.

Double Dutch is always played on hard, flat surfaces such as school or church gymnasium floors. Gym clothes and sneakers are required. Official Double Dutch rope is used. In competitive Double Dutch, ropes, score sheets, mechanical counters, buzzers, and a time clock make up the official equipment list. Training sessions require instruction manuals and films, and all of them are available through the American Double Dutch League.

If you want to get information about Double Dutch and start a program in your neighborhood, at school, or at the recreation center, contact the American Double Dutch League in New York. The League has information on memberships, newsletters, books, training, and competition ropes, and a film.

You also might want to check to see if there is a Double Dutch competition in a city near you. Today more than a quarter of a million kids jump Double Dutch in cities across the country—including New York, Philadelphia, Chicago, Milwaukee, Oakland, and Washington, D.C. It's great fun to watch the kids try to set the world record in singles for fast jumping. Some kids jump hundreds of times in just two minutes!

PRIZES:

Prizes vary from community to community.

Can you tell us how you got started in the activity?

....

"I started in first grade and my uncle holds the world record."

Corey Morning

What do you think we should tell other kids about the contest you won?

....

"It's a fun competitive contest. You're nervous at first, but you'll get used to it."

 Chad Steinmetz

SANDCASTLE CONTESTS

Sandcastle contests are held on beaches all over the country, but they vary as to how they are organized. Sometimes people work alone, sometimes in small groups, and sometimes they work with bulldozers and large groups of people to create huge sand sculptures. More than 20,000 tons of sand were bulldozed by machine and 1,400 people worked to create a gigantic sandcastle at Treasure Island, Florida. At Cabrillo Beach Marine Museum in San Pedro, California, more than 600 people spent 6½ hours building a life-sized sculpture of a whale. They outlined the shape of the whale with a rope and dug a trench about three feet deep around the outline. Then they packed and shaped the sand using boards, shovels, and their hands and feet. The sculptors sprayed the whale with water during the day to keep the sand from drying out. At Ipswich, Massachusetts, small groups and individuals created big sandcastles, modern sculptures, dinosaurs, an Egyptian pyramid, and even a snowman. If you enter a sandcastle contest, you can create whatever you can dream up! Here are some events we've heard about.

Annual Cannon Beach Sandcastle Contest

Cannon Beach Chamber of Commerce
P.O. Box 64
Cannon Beach, OR 97110

WHO CAN ENTER?

Pee Wee: Ages 6 and under
Junior: Younger than high school age

TIME OF YEAR:

May

WHAT IS IT?

Sandcastle Day in Cannon Beach, Oregon, came about because of an earthquake and the resulting tidal wave in 1964. The wall of water washed away a bridge and covered over the lower area of town, causing many people to leave the town of Cannon Beach. To help revive the town, Sandcastle Day was started for children. Today it has become a family event for people of all ages—it has close to 1,000 participants and annually draws 25,000 to 30,000 spectators to the beach.

Starting at 4:30 a.m. on Sandcastle Day, the beach layout crew divides up the area on the beach according to the number of entries in each division. Entry fees are $1 for Pee Wees and $2 for Juniors.

Contestants can start work as early as 7:30 a.m. but must check in by 9:30 a.m. and be ready for judging by 1 p.m. All work must be confined to the plot boundaries, and no sand may be added or removed, but water to help set the sand may be added. Tools, aids, or forms of any sort may be used in the process of construction, but in no way can they support the sand in the finished form. Objects natural to the beach—driftwood, shells, seaweed, etc.—may be used as decoration.

Young children may receive limited advice from adults, but the adults must remain outside rope boundaries. A special learning/teaching plot is set up near headquarters. Teachers are available there to assist youngsters in some of the finer points and techniques of sandcastle building, such as dripping trees and seaweed flags.

PRIZES:

Best Sandcastle Award: Awards in each age division for the best sandcastle

Award of Merit: Each judge gives awards in each age division for design, suitability, and idea selection

Judges' Choice: Each judge gives awards in each age division for outstanding appearance plus teamwork

Promotion of Art In Sand: Award for outstanding artistry in sand

All contestants 12 years and under: Bonus prize bag

The Whale Newspaper Rehoboth Beach Sandcastle Contest

c/o Trish Hogenmiller, Editor
Whale Newspaper
P.O. Box 37
Lewes, DE 19958

WHO CAN ENTER?

Ages 11 and under
Ages 12 and over

TIME OF YEAR:

First Saturday in August

WHAT IS IT?

Give life to your imagination. Make your dreams come true with a sandcastle. Create your fantasy—any shape, anything, anyone—and make it on the beach. The judges will grade sculptures on use of materials, design and engineering, imagination, and visual appeal. It's OK to design with tools, but you can only use things found at the beach.

WHAT ARE MY CHANCES?

In 1990, 18 of the 50 entrants won prizes.

Annual Speed Rope Jumping Contest

Rod Turner
P.O. Box 81
Bloomer, WI 54724

WHO CAN ENTER?

Division I: Girls, Grades 1–2; Boys, Grades 1–2
Division II: Girls, Grades 3–4; Boys, Grades 3–4
Division III: Girls, Grades 5–6; Boys, Grades 5–6
Division IV: Girls, Grades 7–8; Boys, Grades 7–8
Adult Division: Grades 9 and over

TIME OF YEAR:

January

WHAT IS IT?

Speed rope jumpers try to make the most jumps in a 10-second period.

Speed rope jumping is great fun to do with others, but you can practice by yourself. Enjoy the excitement of jumping up and down like a human pogo stick. There are so many ways to jump, and you will discover different ways to keep your balance.

The top five girls and the top five boys in each division of the Annual Speed Rope Jumping Contest go into the finals. Jumpers use a quarter-inch manila rope. No handles or gloves may be used. Each jumper is allowed two tries at making the most jumps within a 10-second period. Your score is the try with the most jumps.

PRIZES:

Grand Champion: Grand Champion Trophy
First and Second Place: Trophies
All finalists: Medallions

WHAT ARE MY CHANCES?

In 1990, 252 people entered, and there were 29 winners.

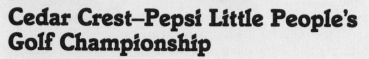

Cedar Crest–Pepsi Little People's Golf Championship

Cedar Crest Country Club
Tournament Headquarters
P.O. Box 3632
Quincy, IL 62305

WHO CAN ENTER?

Ages 3–17 as of the last day of the tournament. There is a boys' tournament and a girls' tournament. In each tournament there are seven divisions:

Division 1: Ages 3–5
Division 2: Ages 6–7
Division 3: Ages 8–9
Division 4: Ages 10–11
Division 5: Ages 12–13
Division 6: Ages 14–15
Division 7: Ages 16–17

TIME OF YEAR:

June

WHAT IS IT?

Kids play golf with other kids their own age. There is also a parent-child tournament.

This golf championship is for kids who know how to play golf. You must register for the tournament by sending an entry fee, a certified copy of your birth certificate, and a picture of yourself. You must also send with these materials a short summary of your golfing history and other interests, both academic and athletic, and your family's involvement in sports. You will need the help of your parents or some other adult to register for this competition. It is important to register as early as possible because the number of players in each division is limited.

This tournament is a four-day event. On the first day the Pepsi parent-child golf events take place. A parent and a kid compete as a team with other parent-kid teams in a golf game. If your parents don't play golf, the officials will help find an adult for you to play with. There are three age groups for the parent-child event: ages 3–7, 8–11, and 12–17.

On the second day, practice rounds are held along with a meeting in which the rules for the tournament are outlined. There is also a picnic dinner and a golf clinic. On the third day the first round of play and a banquet are held, and on the fourth day the final round of play is held and presentation of trophies takes place.

PRIZES:

First, Second, and Third Place in each division: Trophies

First Prize in each division for parent-kid teams: Trophies

Lowest scoring boy and girl in Divisions 3, 4, 5, 6, and 7: $300 in expenses toward any qualifying golf tournament or $300 toward tuition at golf camp, golf school, or college

Each player: Three days' green fees, bag tag, tees, ball markers, Pepsi Little People's golf ball and visor, picnic dinner, banquet, and Pepsi

Great Crate Race

c/o Mrs. Diane Atwood
Dublin Road
South Thomaston, ME 04858

WHO CAN ENTER?

People of any age compete according to their weight.
Lightweight: 0–100 lbs.
Middleweight: 100–150 lbs.
Heavyweight: 150–200 lbs.
Ultra-Heavyweight: Above 200 lbs.

TIME OF YEAR:

July

WHAT IS IT?

Lobster crates are tied together. The crates float on top of the water, and the racers try to balance themselves and run across them as fast as possible.

Can you walk on water? Well, maybe you can by stepping on a row of lobster crates. You will need sneakers, a bathing suit, and balance enough to walk over as many crates as possible before you fall into the water. The Great Crate Race is a crazy way to take a swim but a great way to have some fun. There are many other races across crates in the water, but the Great Crate Race is the world's first!

For the race, 50 lobster crates are tied together between two piers. If you make it across the 50 crates, you have to turn around and come back. The object is to cross as many times as possible without falling off. One girl crossed over 2,300 crates. That means she crossed the 50 crates 46 times!

PRIZES:

First Prize in each weight class: $25
Runners-up in each weight class: Lobster dinner

International Jugglers' Association Competitions

International Jugglers' Association
P.O. Box 29
Kenmore, NY 14217

WHO CAN ENTER?

Nationals: All ages
Juniors: Ages 17 and under
Numbers: Junior and Senior categories
Goggling: Junior and Senior categories

TIME OF YEAR:

Third week in July

WHAT IS IT?

Contestants throw groups of rings, balls, and clubs into the air and juggle them.

Juggling is an art with a fabulous history. Here are some facts:
- Former President Ronald Reagan was pictured in a 1947 issue of *Movie Life* magazine juggling three plates on a Hollywood movie set.
- Among the earliest evidence of juggling are paintings of jugglers found on the walls of the Beni-Hassan tombs on the east bank of the Nile River near Speos Artemidos. They are believed to have been made around 1900 B.C.!
- The 1932 edition of *Ripley's Believe It or Not* credits Tom Redway with juggling five apples without a drop while walking 3½ miles between North New Salem and Orange, Massachusetts.
- As part of his act in the first decade of this century, the world-renowned German "gentleman juggler," Kara, sat on a chair and balanced a full wine glass on three straws on his forehead, at the same time spinning something with the index finger of his left hand and juggling a plate and bottle with his right hand!

Perhaps you'd like to join these famous jugglers by working on an unusual act of your own.

The members of the International Jugglers' Association are a blend of top professionals, avid hobbyists, and enthusiastic beginning jugglers. The Association was begun in 1947 to provide meetings at regular intervals in a friendly atmosphere. Every year since, hundreds of jugglers have gone to national conventions to participate in workshops and championship events and to exchange ideas.

Many members of the Association also belong to local juggling clubs that hold regular meetings and festivals of their own. In each edition of *Jugglers World,* the Association magazine, there are several pages listing local juggling clubs and affiliates. Winners in the local competitions go on to participate in regional mini-conventions, and the regional winners are guaranteed a place at the national competitions.

Juggling competitions cover three events:

Nationals: Each contestant presents an 8-minute act, which is judged on costume, music, presentation, and degree of juggling difficulty.

Juniors: Each contestant presents a 7-minute act, which is judged on costume, music, presentation, and degree of juggling difficulty.

Numbers: There are winners in three divisions: clubs, balls, and rings. The object is to see who can juggle the greatest number of clubs, balls, or rings.

Goggling: Running and juggling at the same time. This is in the *Guinness Book of World Records.*

PRIZES:

Nationals: Medals and money
Juniors: Medals
Numbers: Medals in each division (clubs, balls, and rings)
Goggling: Medals

How did you feel when you won?
....

"Extremely excited, overjoyed, and just about ready to explode."

Issac Whitlach

Morgan Horse Judging Contest

Department of Youth and Education
American Morgan Horse Association
P.O. Box 960
Shelburne, VT 05482

WHO CAN ENTER?

Anyone who belongs to the American Morgan Horse Association, a 4-H club, the FFA, Pony Club, a breed-affiliated club, or a high school or college judging team

There are three age levels: 13 and younger; 14–17; 18–21

TIME OF YEAR:

October

WHAT IS IT?

Participants judge in-hand and performance classes and give reasons for their ratings.

Would you like to be a horse judge? You'll have to learn lots about horses and horse competition. Then you can enter the Morgan Horse Judging Contest. Many previous contest participants have gone on to become official horse judges.

In this contest participants judge in-hand and performance classes. At an in-hand class horses are judged on their "conformation"—how well they are shaped and how good they look when they stand in one place. In the performance classes the horses are judged as they move around and perform certain skills.

The contest participants rate the horses and give reasons for their ratings. Their reasons are scored, and they are given points. The 10 highest points in each age level are given prizes.

PRIZES:

First Place in each category: $100, plaque, ribbon, and magazine subscription
Second Place in each category: $100, plaque, ribbon, and magazine subscription
Third–Tenth Place in each category: Plaque and ribbon

The Most Beautiful Eyes in America Contest

National Society to Prevent Blindness
500 East Remington Road
Schaumburt, IL 60173

WHO CAN ENTER?

Open to all residents of the United States and Puerto Rico

TIME OF YEAR:

Affiliate judging in August
National judging in October

WHAT IS IT?

A contest to pick the most beautiful eyes in America.

Approximately 50,000 people went blind last year. Half of them didn't have to. That's what the National Society to Prevent Blindness is all about—working to prevent blindness. By entering this contest, you will help inform others that blindness can be prevented and that healthy eyes are beautiful eyes.

Established in 1908, the National Society to Prevent Blindness helps to prevent blindness through community services.

To enter the contest, complete an entry form and send it with your photograph to the National Society to Prevent Blindness office near you. Submit a photograph that best displays your beautiful eyes. The photograph may be any size, but it must not be retouched. Color photographs are preferred. Print your name, address, and phone number on the back of the photograph. Eyes are judged on beauty and overall healthy appearance. The rest of the face is covered when the judges look at the photograph.

From the photograph entries, the local judges choose 10 finalists to attend an in-person judging. The winner gets flown to Chicago for the national judging in October.

For more information about the contest and the address of an affiliate office near you, write to the address listed above.

PRIZES:

Affiliate Winners: Local prizes and a trip to Chicago for the national judging

National Winners: Trip for two to Disney World in Orlando, Florida

National Artistic, Speed, and Roller Hockey Championships

United States Amateur Confederation of Roller Skating
7700 A Street
P.O. Box 83067
Lincoln, NB 68501

WHO CAN ENTER?

You must be at least age 6 and be registered with the U.S. Amateur Confederation of Roller Skating.

TIME OF YEAR:

May–October

WHAT IS IT?

There are three different skating events. Each event has a different entry fee and a separate set of rules. The three events are:

1. Speed skating (100, 200, and 300 meters): For ages 6–12
2. Artistic (figure skating, singles skating, pairs skating, and dance): For ages 6 and over
3. Roller hockey (a team sport, played much like ice hockey, only on roller skates): For ages 6 and over

Have you ever watched a roller-skating race and felt the excitement as the skaters raced past one another towards the finish line? Sometimes the excitement in a roller-skating race can be so intense that as an observer you feel like you are in the race yourself. If you prefer a quieter activity, but still like to roller skate, you might enjoy the artistic competition instead. Putting together a choreographed roller-skating routine can be tough work, but being involved can be great.

You must carry your amateur status card with you to the competition and pay the required entry fee.

Each event has many different divisions. You are placed in a division according to your age and skating ability. Your skating ability is determined by the level of U.S. Amateur Confederation of Roller Skating achievement test you pass.

Any member of the U.S. Amateur Confederation can enter a regional skating competition. If you are one of the top three winners at a regional skating championship, you can compete in the national skating competitions.

PRIZES:

National Skating Championship—top three winners: Medals

National Skating Championship (Speed)—Overall Placement Award: Trophy

National Skating Championship (Roller Hockey)—top three winners in each division: Medals and/or trophies

Regional Skating Championships—top three winners: Medals

How did you feel when you won?

....

"I felt so wonderful. I cried, and my mom was so proud she cried, too."

Cadie Morning

National Horseshoe Pitchers Association World Championships

National Horseshoe Pitchers Association
P.O. Box 7927
Columbus, OH 43207

WHO CAN ENTER?

Junior Boys Division: Ages 17 and under as of January 1 of the current year

Junior Girls Division: Ages 17 and under as of January 1 of the current year

TIME OF YEAR:

July and August

WHAT IS IT?

Kids throw horseshoes, trying to make them land around a stake 30 feet away.

Once upon a time, many people thought horseshoes hung over their doors brought them good luck. They hung them pointed ends up so their luck wouldn't run out and so nothing but good luck would come through their door. Not many people do this anymore, but if you look in the country you might see a few leftover ones nailed over the doors of barns and stables and sheds. Of course, for horses, horseshoes have always been lucky. They wear them on the bottoms of their feet so their hooves won't get bruised when they travel over rough places.

But the best way for you to use horseshoes is to throw them around a stake in a game of horseshoes. All you need for the game are two stakes, four horseshoes, and a strong arm! You can even practice at home by yourself, using tree branches as your stakes. With a little luck and lots of practice you could become a horseshoe-pitching champion!

During the World Championships, the horseshoe game is played in the following way. First, there is a preliminary round in which you are matched up with another child in your age division who is fairly equal to you in horseshoe-throwing ability. You and your opponent each throw 50 horseshoes. When you throw the horseshoe and it lands around the stake correctly, it is called a ringer. Your ringer percentage in the preliminary round determines which class you will compete in during the championships.

The 16 kids with the highest ringer percentages from the preliminary round compete against one another in the top class, Championship Class. Then the 12 kids with the next highest ringer percentages from the preliminary round compete in Class A. The rest of the contestants are classified in groups of 12 according to their ringer percentages.

During the championship round, you are matched up with someone in your class. The choice of the first pitch is determined by the toss of a coin or a flipped-up shoe. If you win the coin toss, you throw two horseshoes in a row. You and your partner continue throwing horseshoes until someone scores 40 points. Again, the judges calculate the ringer percentages of all the kids in your class. If you are in the top class and have the best record in the championship round, you will be the World Horseshoe Pitching Champion in your division.

PRIZES:
World Champion: $500 trust fund (amount may vary from year to year) and trophy
Second Place in Championship Class: $300 trust fund and trophy
Third Place in Championship Class: $200 trust fund and trophy
Fourth–Sixteenth Place in Championship Class: Trophies
First, Second, and Third Place in each division: Trophies

How did you find out about the contest?
....

"I belong to the NHPA (National Horseshoe Pitchers Association) and I receive a horseshoe pitchers 'Newsline' each month. I find out about tournaments from it."

Alan Francis

National Rotten Sneaker Championship Sponsored by Odor-Eaters™ Insoles

Montpelier Recreation Department
55 Barre Street
Montpelier, VT 05602

WHO CAN ENTER?

Anyone age 18 or younger

TIME OF YEAR:

First day of spring

WHAT IS IT?

The kid with the rottenest sneakers, which are "rotten through use, not abuse," wins.

HOLD IT! Don't throw away your rotten old sneakers... yet! And don't let your mother, grandmother, aunt, or big sister—all people who are great at getting rid of all worn-out (to them) things—throw them out, either.

Those old, smelly sneakers might win you a prize and a smidgen of publicity if you can just hang onto them a little bit longer. You wouldn't want to give up being the Odor-Eaters™ Rotten Sneaker Champion of your city or town, now, would you?

What is the Odor-Eaters™ Rotten Sneaker Championship and how do you get into it? Well... it all began in 1976 when a local store owner wanted to take a picture of a "rotten" pair of sneakers to use as an advertisement. So he and a newspaper photographer went to the Montpelier Recreation Department gym to see what they could find. They found exactly what they were looking for—a kid with a very rotten pair of sneakers. The photographer took a picture of that kid's sneakers, and that's how this contest began.

If you have a pair of rotten sneakers you would like to enter in this contest, here are some rules you must follow:
1. You must wear your sneakers and keep them on your feet during judging.
2. You may enter one pair of sneakers only.
3. Sneakers must be naturally worn and torn, not purposely cut or abused.

4. Sneakers must fit your feet.

This is a two-part contest, beginning with the National Championship. That is immediately followed by the International final, which includes all the regional winners.

You must register for this contest by calling the Montpelier Recreation Department or by sending in a registration form. It is important to register as early as possible because this contest is limited to the first 50 entries. You must show up at the Montpelier Recreation Department on the first day of spring wearing your rotten sneakers.

Suppose you don't live near Vermont, but would like to enter the Odor-Eaters™ Rotten Sneaker Championship anyway. Write to:

Julie Bohl
Rotten Sneaker Coordinator
Odor-Eaters™ Insoles
P.O. Box 328 RSM
White Plains, NY 10602

Julie will let you know if there is a regional contest that will be held in your area. If you would like to hold your own Odor-Eaters™ Rotten Sneaker Championship, just find an adult to help you set it up. Then write to Julie at the address above, and she'll send you a manual on how to hold one.

At the Odor-Eaters™ International Rotten Sneaker Contest there are six expert judges who ask all the kids who enter to walk across a stage. The judges will ask them to run in place, jump, and perform other simple feats to make sure their sneakers stay on. The kids will also be asked to move their feet so the judges can examine the sneakers, which are judged in eight categories: soles, laces or velcro closing, eyelets, tongue, toe, heel, overall condition, and the judges' favorite—odor. The judges give a score of one to five in each category, and the "rottenest" pair of sneakers—those with the lowest score—is the champion.

PRIZES:

Grand Prize Winner: $500 U.S. savings bond, a trophy, and a "Sneaker Survival Kit." This kit includes a brand-new pair of sneakers, laces, Odor-Eaters™ insoles, and a Rotten Sneaker contest T-shirt. The winning pair of sneakers will be enshrined in the Odor-Eaters™ Hall of Fumes, and the winner's name will be engraved on a permanent plaque in the Montpelier Department of Recreation.

Four Finalists: U.S. savings bonds, trophies, and "Sneaker Survival Kits"

World Footbag Association Contests

World Footbag Association
1317 Washington Avenue, Suite 7
Golden, CO 80401

WHO CAN ENTER?

Junior Division: Ages 15 and under

TIME OF YEAR:

All year-round

WHAT IS IT?

Footbag is a modern version of ancient kicking games. For footbag competitions, the small footbags are kept in the air only with the feet and lower body, except in the freestyle events, in which the upper body may be used.

What is a footbag—a bag full of feet? Nonsense! A footbag is round, smaller than a baseball, and is usually made with a leather surface. It is hard, but soft enough so you can kick it without hurting yourself.

You throw a baseball, but you kick a footbag. Soccer balls are for kicking, but the reason for kicking a footbag is different. For example, you can try to keep it in the air with your kicks. See how long you can do it without the footbag touching the ground. A 15-year-old boy kicked a footbag 7,138 times in a row. This means it did not touch the ground between kicks. It took him 1 hour and 14 minutes to do it!

Footbag is something you can practice alone, but it's more fun to play with others. Often a circle of players is formed, and the players kick the footbag back and forth. Anybody is welcome in a circle, so the better players help the novices. It's fun to see how many times you can kick the footbag before it hits the ground. The more skilled you become, the more interesting routines you can do with others.

In footbag competitions, there may be four events:

Footbag Consecutive

This game is simple. You keep the footbag in the air for as long as possible using only your feet and knees. No contact above the waist is allowed. One point is awarded for each kick. You may compete in singles and doubles footbag consecutive.

Footbag Freestyle

Footbag freestyle allows you to create artistic routines. In freestyle competitions you combine tricks, cooperative, and dancelike movements into routines that are often done to music. In competition, only footbag freestyle allows you to use your upper body.

Footbag Golf

Footbag golf is played like standard golf. Players start by teeing off, kick the footbag through and around various hazards, and end by kicking the footbag into a marked area.

Footbag Net

Footbag net combines kicks and fancy footwork. Scoring rules are the same as in volleyball, and the playing rules are like tennis. There are singles and doubles competitions.

For $1 you can become a life member of the World Footbag Association. You will receive a players' manual, which tells you how to set up a footbag club or competition. You will also receive a copy of *Footbag World,* the association's magazine, which will give you news about when touring teams of footbag players are likely to be in your area. Maybe the college near you has a footbag team or events. Maybe the state fair does, too.

PRIZES:

Junior Footbag Consecutive: Ribbon or plaque
Junior Footbag Freestyle: Ribbon or plaque
Junior Footbag Golf: Ribbon or plaque
Junior Footbag Net: Ribbon or plaque

World Junior Frisbee® Disc Contests®

Wham-O, Inc.
835 East El Monte Street, P.O. Box 4
San Gabriel, CA 91775

WHO CAN ENTER?

Boys: Ages 11 and under; ages 12–15
Girls: Ages 11 and under; ages 12–15

TIME OF YEAR:

Community: To be completed by July 21
Regional: To be completed by August 10
World Finals: In this contest, you throw a Frisbee for distance or for accuracy, or make special catches. If you reach the finals, there are more events. They're described below.

WHAT IS IT?

If you're really good at Frisbee, this is the contest for you. Each year Wham-O, the company that makes Frisbees, sponsors a World Junior Frisbee® Disc Contest® for kids 15 and under. There are three levels to this competition. You start in a community contest and, if you win enough points, you can advance to the regional contests and then on to the World Finals. From the regional finals only the top girl and boy advance to the World Finals.

Both the community and regional contests include three different events. First is the distance throwing event, in which you win points for throwing a Frisbee long distances. Second is the accuracy event, in which you try to throw a Frisbee at a target from various distances and angles. Third is the catching event, in which you try to make different kinds of catches, like behind-the-back or between-the-legs catches. In the World Finals, there are also "maximum time aloft," disc golf, and freestyle events. In the freestyle event the contestant performs a three-minute routine of tricks to music.

PRIZES:
World Finals
First Prize: $1,000 U.S. savings bonds to winning boy and girl
Second Prize: $500 U.S. savings bonds to winning boy and girl
Third Prize: $250 U.S. savings bonds to winning boy and girl

Regional Contests

First Prize in each category: $100 U.S. savings bond, commemorative award, and certificate

Other top finishers: Certificates

Community contests: Commemorative awards and certificates

What did you like best about this contest?

. . . .

"The people who play Frisbee are all a big family of friends."

Shawn Kennedy

CHAPTER 5

Far-Out Contests and Fabulous Fairs

There are hundreds, maybe even thousands, of fairs throughout the U.S. each year. They range from small local fairs, like a school, club, or church fair, to county fairs to special-interest fairs to gigantic state fairs. Some of them are held in connection with special holidays—the Fourth of July, Halloween, or Easter, for instance. County and state fairs are usually held in late summer and were originally meant to celebrate the end of harvest. Most county and state fairs still have many exhibits having to do with farm animals, home-grown fruits and vegetables, and homemade jams, pies, cakes, etc.

Almost every fair will have a number of contests that children can enter. Many of these contests are just for fun and require no special skills—watermelon seed spitting, for instance—others are more serious and require a lot of talent, time, and patience—like raising chickens or growing prize-winning vegetables.

We have described just a few fairs and festivals in this chapter, to give you an idea of what's available. Unless you happen to live nearby, you probably won't be able to go to any of them, but there are sure to be fairs in your area. You may also get some good ideas on contests that you and your friends, or your school, could run.

To get more information about fairs in your area, contact your state department of tourism, county or state fair office, or your state association of fairs and festivals. Your local newspaper may also have listings.

Annual Surf Fishing Tournament

Bethany-Fenwick Area Chamber of Commerce
P.O. Box 881
Bethany Beach, DE 19930

WHO CAN ENTER?

Ages 9 and under
Ages 10–14

TIME OF YEAR:

October

WHAT IS IT?

Surf fishing is fishing in the ocean in shallow water or on sand bars near the shoreline, not from a boat or pier.

This contest gives you a chance to enjoy the beach and water while you fish. You can have a picnic, too. Imagine the excitement of catching a bluefish all by yourself.

There are different fees for individuals and families. To enter this contest, you need the following equipment:

- Fishing rod with surf or spinning tackle only—no more than two rods allowed
- Fishing line—linen, nylon, dacron, or monofilament
- Sinker—no weight limit
- Bait—no restrictions, but you will have to supply your own
- Artificial lures are permitted. (Lures are attached to the fishing line to attract fish.)

The rules of the beach are:

1. No wet lines before the start.
2. Fishing only at designated times and areas.
3. You must bait and cast your own rod and remove your own fish.
4. Fish must be caught on hook or lure and landed on the beach.
5. The person who hooks a fish while standing in the surf or at an outer sand bar must bring the fish to the main beach.
6. Points are given for the length of fish, measured from tip to tip. Different points are also given for different kinds of fish.
7. The total number of points determines the winner.

PRIZES:

Most points: $500

Second most points: $350

Largest individual fish: $250

Most points for children ages 9 and under: Surf rod and reel

Most points for children ages 10–14: Surf rod and reel

Easter Promenade

Rehoboth Beach–Dewey Beach Chamber of Commerce
P.O. Box 216
Rehoboth Beach, DE 19971

WHO CAN ENTER?

Boys and girls can enter the "Best Dressed" contest in these age categories: Ages 1–4; Ages 5–9; Ages 10–15; Couples of all ages

TIME OF YEAR:

Easter Sunday from 1:00 to 3:00 p.m.

WHAT IS IT?

It's a chance to show off special spring clothes and bonnets.

Over 800 people of all ages attend the Easter Promenade. For each event the participants go up on the stage so that the judges and the audience can get a good look at them. Other age groups can enter the contest—we only listed the kids' categories above. There is special children's judging on attire and store-bought or homemade bonnets.

There is also entertainment and the chance to have your picture taken with the Easter Bunny. Contestants hope that warm weather will add to the fun in what is "The Nation's Summer Capital."

In October, Rehoboth Beach holds a Sea Witch Weekend Festival. It includes a Bubble Gum Blowing Contest, a Broom Throwing Contest, and other fun stuff.

PRIZES:

First Prize in each category: Trophy

Frog Festival

Rayne Chamber of Commerce and Agriculture
P.O. Box 383
Rayne, LA 70578

TIME OF YEAR:

September

WHAT IS IT?

Every year, guests at the Frog Festival enjoy a truly unique celebration in which frogs are the stars of the show in many contests.

Rayne, Louisiana, is in the heart of Cajun country, where people who are a mixture of French, Creole, and American speak a unique brand of English with lots of French mixed in. The Frog Festival is meant to celebrate the superior bullfrogs of the region and the unusual heritage of its people. The festival consists of both scheduled and spontaneous events. Among the contests that are popular yearly favorites are the frog racing and jumping events, the frog eating contest, and a number of beauty contests from the Diaper Derby to Little Mr. and Miss Tadpole to the Junior Frog Festival Queen. Here are some of the contests in which children can participate.

Frog Jump

WHO CAN ENTER?

Ages 11 and under
Ages 12 and over

WHAT IS IT?

For the frog jump, each frog is permitted three jumps, and then the distance is measured from the starting point to the point where the frog lands on the third jump. The frog is placed in the starting circle, and no one may touch the frog after its first jump unless the frog is disqualified. The contestant may jump up and down, shout, blow on the frog, or do anything else to get him to jump. Each frog will be allowed 15 seconds for each jump. If it does not jump within the allowed time it will be disqualified. See below for further contest rules.

PRIZES:

First, Second, and Third prizes: Trophy

Frog Race

WHO CAN ENTER?

Ages 11 and under
Ages 12 and over

WHAT IS IT?

The frogs will be raced in heats. Each contestant will be assigned a numbered lane. The frog will be allowed 60 seconds to reach the finish line, which will be 20 feet from the starting blocks. Each winning frog in a particular heat will advance to the finals.

The rules for both the Frog Jump and Frog Race contests are:
1. Fees for Jump or Race for children will be $1.
2. Frog rental will be $1.
3. If you race or jump your own bullfrog, spring frog, or toad, it must measure 4 inches from head to tail.
4. All frogs must be named in order to prevent "frog calling" confusion.
5. No contestant may feed a frog Tabasco sauce or other Louisiana hot sauce to make the frog jump farther.
6. No contestant may feed an opponent's frog Louisiana rice or soybeans to slow down the frog.

PRIZES:

First, Second, and Third prizes: Trophy
News Media Contest: Trophy

Jr. Frog Festival Queen's Contest

WHO CAN ENTER?

Girls ages 9 and 10

WHAT IS IT?

Entrants will be judged on poise, beauty, and conversational ability.

PRIZES:

First Place: Crown, banner, and trophy
Second and Third places: Banner and trophy

Gilroy Garlic Festival

Gilroy Garlic Festival Association, Inc.
P.O. Box 2311
Gilroy, CA 95021

Every year, the people in Gilroy, California, hold a great festival in celebration of garlic, that wonderful—but smelly—herb. There's always lots of good food and musical entertainment at this festival and a number of special events. In past years there have been golf and tennis tournaments, runs, a garlic braiding contest, a beauty contest to pick the Garlic Queen, and a garlic cooking contest. One good event for kids to enter, especially kids who are serious bikers, is the Tour de Garlique.

Tour de Garlique

WHO CAN ENTER?

All ages

TIME OF YEAR:

Midsummer's Harvest Celebration in July

WHAT IS IT?

The Tour de Garlique is a multilevel bicycle tour that includes a 20-mile family route, a brisk 110-km route through Cienega Valley, a challenging 100-mile route looping through the Pinnacles National Monument, and a 200-km route with an early morning climb up Fremont Peak. Kids usually participate in the 20-mile ride.

Riders will be supplied with detailed route maps, clearly marked routes, rest stops, lunch, and extra water stops. And of course there are gobs of great eats: fresh fruits, sandwiches, and munchies, with ice cream at the finish. The weather may be hot, so carry an extra water bottle.

The rules of the Tour are:
1. Ride safely and obey all traffic laws.
2. All bicycles will be inspected for safe operation. Only those that pass inspection are allowed on the course.
3. Hardshell helmets are required.
4. Bring spare money, tube patch kit, pump, and water bottle.

5. Notify a Tour official if abandoning the tour.
6. Course closes at 6 p.m.; riders must exit if not finished by then.
7. Riders under 18 years of age must carry a medical authorization form signed by a parent or legal guardian.
8. The ride goes on rain or shine.
9. Entry fees vary according to which race you enter. There are family rates for the 20-mile tour. If you plan to enter, it is best to contact the Gilroy Garlic Festival early in June.

PRIZES:

All entrants receive a patch and a pass to the Gilroy Garlic Festival.

International Pancake Day of Liberal, Inc. 🐝🐝

P.O. Box 665
505 N. Kansas
Liberal, KS 67905

TIME OF YEAR:
Around Shrove Tuesday, the day before Lent

WHAT IS IT?
International Pancake Day is a three-day celebration in Liberal, Kansas, centered around the centuries-old holiday traditionally held on the Tuesday before Ash Wednesday. There are many activities for families and contests for kids and grown-ups.

The "Pancake Hub of the Universe"! Do you know where it is? Liberal, Kansas! The town of Liberal got this name because every year, on a day chosen to be International Pancake Day, adults and children participate in contests that require them to do something special with pancakes: eat them, flip them, or run with them. You may not be able to eat 62 pancakes in seven minutes like the world record pancake eater but you could become a local celebrity by breaking a pancake record set by another child. And you don't have to go to Liberal, Kansas, to do it. With help from your parents and friends you could organize a Pancake Day to be held in your own hometown. We describe four of the kids' contests below.

Pancake Day Amateur Contest

WHO CAN ENTER?
Tiny Tot: Ages 5–8
Junior: Ages 9–12
Intermediate: Ages 13–16

WHAT IS IT?
This contest is open to all nonprofessional entertainers. First you have preliminary auditions, and then you can compete in the finals. Each act is limited to a maximum of three minutes.

PRIZES:

Tiny Tot
First Prize: $35 and trophy
Second Prize: $25 and trophy
Third Prize: $15 and trophy

Junior
First Prize: $35 and trophy
Second Prize: $25 and trophy
Third Prize: $15 and trophy

Intermediate
First Prize: $50 and trophy
Second Prize: $30 and trophy
Third Prize: $20 and trophy

What do you think we should tell other kids about the contest you won?

....

"It was a lot of fun and it was really neat knowing we were being taped by a TV station. Then I got to see myself on TV that night."

Robbie Lanning

Pancake Eating Contest

WHO CAN ENTER?

Junior Division: Ages 10 and under
Intermediate Division: Ages 11–15

WHAT IS IT?

In this contest you try to eat as many 7-inch pancakes as you can in thirty minutes. The kid who eats the most pancakes is the winner. The rules for the contest are:

1. Once you sit down to the table, you cannot get up for thirty minutes. This includes using the bathroom.
2. Contestants will not be allowed to have assistants.
3. You are disqualified if you throw up the pancakes you have eaten.
4. You can eat your pancakes plain or with anything you want on top. Butter, sugar, and syrup will be provided.

PRIZES:

First Place: Trophy or plaque
Second and Third places: Certificate

Pancake Flip Off

WHO CAN ENTER?

Division I: Ages 10–16
Division II: Ages 17 and over

WHAT IS IT?

In this contest you try to flip as many pancakes as you can in a two-minute time period. Skillets and pancakes will be provided by contest officials. First there is a round of heats in which you compete against other kids who are flipping pancakes at the same time. You will be assigned a counter, who will count how many flips you do in a two-minute time period. If you are one of the winners in the round of heats, you will compete against the other winners in the next round. The kid who does the most pancake flips during the second round is the winner. Recent winners have flipped between 200 and 270 pancakes in two minutes!

PRIZES:

First Place: Plaque
Second and Third places: Certificate

Pancake Race

WHO CAN ENTER?

Elementary I Division: Kindergarten–Grade 3
Elementary II Division: Grades 4–6

WHAT IS IT?

For the Pancake Race, all entrants must wear an apron and head scarf, and carry a small skillet. All entrants must flip their pancake two times. The first flip is to be made immediately after the starting signal and the second flip after the contestant crosses the finish line, to show the pancake is still in the skillet. If the pancake is dropped at any time, the contestant may pick it up and place it back in the skillet and continue the race. Any assistance from spectators or any other persons will automatically disqualify contestants.

PRIZES:

First Prize: Trophy
Second and Third prizes: Certificate

What did you like about the contest?

....

"When they gave me my plaque. It was different sitting beside kids that ate too much and they got sick in their buckets and I was hoping they wouldn't make me sick."

Robbie Lanning

Jumping Frog Jubilee

Calaveras County Fair
39th District Agricultural Association
P.O. Box 96
Angels Camp, CA 95222

WHO CAN ENTER?
Junior Division: Ages 11 and under

TIME OF YEAR:
Third weekend in May

WHAT IS IT?
Kids put frogs on a pad and try to coach them to jump the farthest. We've already described one frog jumping contest (at the Rayne, Louisiana, Frog Festival), but we had to tell you about this one, too, because this is the one that Mark Twain wrote about in his famous story, "The Celebrated Jumping Frog of Calaveras County." This frog contest also has the biggest prizes of any such contest in the United States.

For this contest we have included lots of facts about frogs:
- Different types of frogs make different sounds, including croaking, whistling, snoring, clicking, chirping, trilling, and grunting.
- Frogs come out of hibernation when the temperature warms up. If a frog should go to sleep somewhere where it does not warm up, in a deep well or cave, for instance, it may hibernate for years.
- The loud croaking sounds of frogs are usually made by the males and can be made both under water and out of water.
- Frogs have a highly developed sense of touch but not much sense of taste. They eat live worms and insects.

When you train your frog to jump far, you are a frog jockey. This job has you doing whatever it takes to get your frog jumping. You can stomp up and down, yell, make funny noises, make funny faces, and talk to your frog. Remember, however, to be gentle with your frog when you are handling it.
The rules for the contest are:
1. All frogs must be registered.

2. You cannot enter or jump more than 10 frogs per day.
3. All qualifying trials and the final jump are held on the frog stages.
4. Each frog is allowed 15 seconds on each jump. If the frog does not jump in that time, it is disqualified.
5. After a frog is placed in the starting circle, no one may touch it after the first jump.
6. Length of jump is measured in a straight line from the starting point to the point of landing.
7. Frogs must be 4 inches in length, from nose to tail. Important: If you don't have a frog you can "rent" one. Also, a "jockey" is provided for you if you wish.
8. The current world-record holder is "Rosie the Ribiter," jumped by Lee Giudici of Santa Clara, California. The record is 21 feet, 5¾ inches.

The top three frogs in the Junior Division are eligible to jump in the Grand Finals.

PRIZES:

Any frog that sets a new world's record: $1,500
Any winning frog in the Grand Finals that equals the world's record: $600
Grand Finals winner: $500
Second Prize: $300
Third Prize: $150
Fourth Prize: $75
Fifth Prize: $50
Sixth Prize: $25
Seventh Prize: $15
Eighth Prize: $10

Junior Chili Cookoff

Republic of Texas Chilympiad
P.O. Box 188
San Marcos, TX 78667

WHO CAN ENTER?

Children in Grades 1–12 can enter the Chili Competition and the Showmanship Competition.

TIME OF YEAR:

Sunday of the third weekend in September

WHAT IS IT?

Contestants cook chili, and the best-tasting chili wins the prizes.

Join the Republic of Texas Chilympiad for three days of chili madness featuring the Texas Men's State Championship Chili Cookoff, the world's largest and most spectacular chili cook-off. For the Chili Competition, all chili must be cooked on site the day of the cook-off from scratch. "Scratch" is defined as starting with raw meat. Regular commercial chili powder is permissible, but complete commercial chili mixes are not permitted. All spices are subject to inspection by the judging committee and/or by a member of the Regional Referees.

A blind system of judging is used. A judging cup will be brought to all contestants. The cup is prepared with two separate but matching numbers: one number is concealed on the bottom of the cup and the other number is on a piece of paper inside the cup. This second numbered paper must be signed and kept by the contestant. There will be no record kept of the number. The finished chili is turned in to the judging area in the cup with the concealed number. After final judging is complete and the winning samples determined, the concealed numbers on the winners' cups will be called out. To claim their awards, winners must present the papers with matching numbers.

In the Showmanship Competition, awards are given to cook-off sites based on theme, costume, booth setup, action, and audience participation.

PRIZES:

Chili Competition
Top three winners: Trophy
Top ten winners: Name printed in local newspaper

Showmanship Competition
Top three winners: Trophy

What do you think we should tell other kids about the contest you won?
....

"It is fun and exciting, but it takes work and patience."

Denise Schulze

How did you find out about the contest?
....

"My dad started cooking in the senior (adult) cook-offs and then the people who organize the cook-offs started having junior cook-offs."

Cathy West

Junior World Championship Duck Calling Contest

Stuttgart Chamber of Commerce
P.O. Box 932
Stuttgart, AR 72160

WHO CAN ENTER?

Ages up to 14 as of the hour of the contest are eligible. A birth certificate must be submitted at the time of registration as proof of stated age.

TIME OF YEAR:

Thanksgiving weekend

WHAT IS IT?

You use a duck call (a special whistle) to make different kinds of sounds that will call ducks.

Imagine you are in a remote wild game reservation area and are surrounded by tall trees and ponds. You make your way toward a rice field near a lake and in the distance you spot a duck. Kneeling in the grass, you begin your duck call. Imagine the thrill of seeing the duck change its flying direction and come toward you. Using a duck call is also a good way of staying in touch with any person who may be a distance from you—you can call your friend with the duck call.

To call a duck you will need a duck call. This is a wooden cylinder 5 inches long that has a reed in its hollow center. When you blow into the mouthpiece, air goes across the reed and makes a sound like a quacking duck. For a contest, you will need to learn to make some of the following calls: hail or long distance call, mating or lonesome call, feed or chatter call, and comeback call.

In a duck calling contest, the decision of the judges shall be based on the total score. Each contestant shall be allowed a maximum of 90 seconds. When you win an official regional duck calling contest, you can then participate in the World Championship Duck Calling Contest.

PRIZES:

Winner: Named the Junior World Champion Duck Caller; cash and prizes
First, Second, and Third Runners-Up: Cash and prizes

Lakeview Chamber of Commerce Sled Dog Races

Lakeview Chamber of Commerce
Lakeview, OR 97630

WHO CAN ENTER?

Pee Wee (1 dog): Ages 4–10
Novice (2 dog): Ages 10–12
Novice (3 dog): Ages 12 and up

TIME OF YEAR:

January to March

WHAT IS IT?

Kids race sled dogs over a course for the fastest time.

Would you like to be a musher and shout "Hike!" on a cold winter's day? A musher is a sled dog racer. To sled dogs the word "hike" means "go." The musher stands on a special sled. The dogs wear harnesses and are attached to the sled with ropes. When they hear the word "hike" they're off and running. The musher holds on to the sled as the dogs pull it over a marked race course. After a fast and exciting ride the musher shouts "Whoa!," and the dogs stop running. The musher and dog team that finish the course in the shortest amount of time are winners.

Many towns, chambers of commerce, and ski areas in the United States and Canada hold sled dog races during the winter. Anyone in the family can enter in the division of their age category. In the Pee Wee division one dog pulls the musher and sled 100 yards (91 m) then turns around and goes back. In the Novice 2 division two dogs pull a musher and sled over the same course. In the Novice 3 division three dogs pull the musher and sled over a 1 mile (1.6 km) course. There are a variety of races for adults, too.

PRIZES:

Prizes vary from year to year and race to race; usually include trophies and dog food

Logan County Fair

P.O. Box 950
Sterling, CO 80751

TIME OF YEAR:
August

WHAT IS IT?
The Logan County Fair is a great fair with many contests, but we are listing only those that are very unusual.

Cricket Races

WHO CAN ENTER?
Peewee Cricketeers: Ages 7 and under
Junior Cricketeers: Ages 8–10
Senior Cricketeers: Ages 11–13

WHAT IS IT?
When you enter you can race either one or two crickets. Crickets are placed in the center of a measured, circular race course. The cricket jumping out of the circle the fastest is the winner.

PRIZES:
Grand Champion Cricketeer: Trophy from Kiwanis Club
First Prize: $2.00
Second Prize: $1.50
Third Prize: $1.00
Fourth Prize: 50¢
Fifth Prize: Ribbon

Pet Rock Show and Race

WHO CAN ENTER?

Best Dressed Division: Ages 10 and under; Ages 10–13; Ages 14–18
Racing Division: Ages under 10; Ages 10–13; Ages 14–18

WHAT IS IT?

Dress up your pet rock for a contest or race it down a plank. No matter where you live—in a house or a houseboat, in a condo or a cottage, in an apartment or with your Great-aunt Agatha who is allergic to cats, dogs, and canaries—you can have a pet.

You won't need a pooper-scooper or a sandbox for this pet. This pet won't lick your face when you're sad or come running to meet you when you come home from school. But a pet rock is a convenient kind of pet to have. You can take it on a vacation with you or leave it at home. You can carry it around in your pocket or hide it away in your top bureau drawer. You can even enter it in a contest like the ones described below. Maybe everybody should have a pet rock.

Rocks entered in these contests must be mature in body and form. They must weigh at least two ounces and not more than five pounds. Rocks entered in the Best Dressed Division may be dressed in human-made materials or decorative paints. Rocks entered in the Racing Division must race without clothing or other props. They will compete from a standing start. A plank 1 by 12 inches and 12 feet long is built on a stand 2½ inches high, with a holding spot at the top for one rock. Each rock must roll down the plank without falling off the edge. The rock must also keep to a course that doesn't interfere with the other rocks. The rock traveling the longest straight line from start to stop will be the winner. Decisions of the judges are final. Sound like fun? It is.

PRIZES:

Grand Champion Racing Rock: Plaque from Kiwanis Club
Grand Champion Pet Rock: Plaque from Kiwanis Club

Prizes in each division at each age level:

First Place: $2.00, plaque, and ribbon
Second Place: $1.50 and ribbon
Third Place: $1.00 and ribbon
Fourth Place: 50¢ and ribbon
Fifth Place: Ribbon

The Friendly Dog's "Tail-Wagging" Contest

WHO CAN ENTER?

Open to all dogs, but they must compete in the same class. No dog shall be discriminated against on the basis of age, color, sex, size, pedigree, or origin. Bob-tailed and no-tail dogs are recognized as handicapped, but don't receive special consideration.

WHAT IS IT?

Most people love a friendly tail-wagging dog. Some dogs' tails wag so fast, you get dizzy watching them. Other tails sway back and forth very slowly. No matter what kind of tail your dog has, you will probably come away from this contest with a better understanding of the body language of dogs.

Dogs must register with their owners or handlers. They must keep their owners or handlers on a leash, unless otherwise directed. Growling at the judges and spectators will be considered bad manners. If a dog bites, it is immediately disqualified. The winners are the dogs able to wag their tails in the friendliest way.

PRIZES:

Champion Wagger: Trophy from Equitable Savings and Loan Association
First Prize: $2.00
Second Prize: $1.50
Third Prize: $1.00
Fourth Prize: 50¢
Fifth Prize: Ribbon

Maine Common Ground Country Fair

Maine Organic Farmers and Gardeners Association
P.O. Box 2176
Augusta, ME 04330

TIME OF YEAR:

September

WHAT IS IT?

The Maine Organic Farmers and Gardeners Association is a group of many people who care about food, fiber, and fuel. The fair is their celebration of country work and country life. It's a great country fair for the whole family.

The fair has a wide variety of family entertainment, including a special entertainment schedule for children on each of the three days. Performers over the years have included storytellers, clowns, mimes, magicians, a one-man band, and dancers. You can see Bruce the Moose, the Puppet Truck, and the Potato Garden Puppet Theater. Some of the well-known performers who have entertained at children's entertainment events have been Jud the Jester, Sam Kilbourne the Pantoclown, and Jackson Gillman.

Kids are a part of the show. You can make pottery, paper, or collages. You can sing, dance, call advice to other performers, or find yourself asked to be on stage with the performer. This is a lot more exciting than television. There are also beginner acts for children who wish to entertain for the first time in their lives. This means that you can plan your very own act or performance. How's that for something exciting to work on?

There are many exhibits and contests at the fair, including a Fiddling Contest and an Open Youth Horse Show. Two of the other contests are described below.

Exhibition Hall Entry Classes

WHO CAN ENTER?

Maine residents of all ages

WHAT IS IT?

This is a chance to show off the giant vegetable you grew in your garden this year. There are many categories for the Exhibition Hall Entry Classes: The Biggest Beet Contest; The Biggest Cabbage Contest; The Biggest Squash Contest; The Giant Cuke Contest; The Great Carrot Contest; The Great Pumpkin Contest; The Great Zucchini Contest; and The Whatever Contest. All entries will be judged by weight.

PRIZES:

Ribbons

Junior Manure Pitch-Off

WHO CAN ENTER?

Ages 14 and under

WHAT IS IT?

For the manure pitch-off, contestants have four tasks: to spear a shovelful of manure and pitch it into a bushel basket 15 feet away; to hurl a shovelful as far as possible; to spread a wheelbarrow load of manure evenly over a 10-by-20-foot area; and to spread as much manure in 3½ minutes as possible.

PRIZES:

Ribbons

What do you think we should tell other kids about the contest you won?

....

"Even if you don't win and you did your best, you're still a winner."

Jenni Strunk

Morton Pumpkin Festival

415 West Jefferson Street
Morton, IL 61550

TIME OF YEAR:
September

WHAT IS IT?

Morton, Illinois, calls itself the "Pumpkin Capital of the World," and each September it celebrates the maturing of the pumpkin with a festival that includes contests for children.

At the Morton Pumpkin Festival, the entire family can enjoy carnival rides, foot races, food and merchants' tents, art and garden shows, pie eating contests, and pumpkins, pumpkins, pumpkins. The food is unbelievable. Butterfly pork chops and pumpkin pie, pumpkin ice cream, pumpkin pancakes, and pumpkin chili are only a few of the pumpkin foods available. For runners of all ages, there is a 2K Fun Run and a 10K. Here are some of the other contests you can enter:

Giant Open Pumpkin Contest

WHO CAN ENTER?
All ages

WHAT IS IT?

No matter where you live, if you have a big beautiful pumpkin growing in your backyard you may enter it in the Giant Open Pumpkin Contest. One year the winning pumpkin weighed 205 pounds! (Morton children can also enter their pumpkins in the giant "king" and "queen" or "tiniest all-orange" pumpkin contests.)

PRIZES:
Biggest Pumpkin: 25¢ per pound awarded to grower

Grand Opening Balloon Release

WHO CAN ENTER?

All ages

WHAT IS IT?

For the Balloon Release you must fill out a card and take it to the Pumpkin Festival grounds on the opening day of the Festival. Your card will be attached to a helium-filled balloon, which you will release. The person whose name is on the card returned from the farthest distance wins a prize and so does the person who returns it.

PRIZES:

Person with balloon traveling farthest: $25
Person returning card: $10

Pie Eating Contest

WHO CAN ENTER?

Ages 8 and under
Ages 9–12
Ages 13–19

WHAT IS IT?

In this contest, you win by eating the most pumpkin pie. Money is hidden in selected pies, so watch out!

PRIZES:

Prizes vary from year to year.

Pumpkin Cookery Contest

WHO CAN ENTER?

Junior Division: Ages up to 18

WHAT IS IT?

There are six categories in the Pumpkin Cookery Contest: main dishes, appetizers, cookies, cakes, breads, and pies. All entries must contain at least ½ cup pumpkin. A limit of two entries in each category will be accepted from each participant. All entries must include two printed or typed copies of the recipe on 4-by-6-inch cards. You must prepare your entry for display and include one portion wrapped separately for the judges to sample.

PRIZES:

First Prize in each category: $50 and ribbon
Second Prize in each category: $20 and ribbon
Third Prize in each category: $10 and ribbon

Pumpkin Decorating Contest

WHO CAN ENTER?

Ages 4 and under; Ages 5–6; Ages 7–8; Ages 9–10; Ages 11–18; Ages over 18; Family Division

WHAT IS IT?

For this contest you can enter your pumpkin fixed up any way you like as long as your decoration follows the theme of the year. For example, in 1990 the theme was "We're Off to See the Pumpkins." Carving the pumpkin is discouraged because it spoils too quickly. You must decorate your entry yourself, unless you are entering the pumpkin in the Family Division. Then your whole family can join in. You will get a free pumpkin to work on for the contest.

PRIZES:

Grand Prize: $50 U.S. savings bond
First Prize in each division: Cash (amount varies from year to year)

Pumpkin Princess Pageant

WHO CAN ENTER?

Girls ages 5 and 6

WHAT IS IT?

In this contest you must wear a costume to fit the theme of the Pageant. Past themes have been "Pumpkins Go Hollywood," "Pumpkins Go for the Gold," and "Pumpkins Around the World." The contestants arrive at the Pageant dressed in their costumes and tell the judges what their costumes mean. They also sing their favorite songs plus a group song such as "If You're Happy and You Know It." The girls are also honored at a Princess Tea and join in the Children's Parade and the Festival Parade.

PRIZES:

First Prize: Trophy and personal banner

National Tom Sawyer Days

Hannibal Jaycees
P.O. Box 230
Hannibal, MO 63401

TIME OF YEAR:
Around the Fourth of July

WHAT IS IT?
National Tom Sawyer Days is one of the best-known Fourth of July celebrations in America. Each year the Tom Sawyer Days are highlighted by the Fence Painting Contest. The contest has been going on for 30 years and is even sanctioned by the United States Congress. Other contests at the National Tom Sawyer Days are the Tomboy Sawyer, and Tom Sawyer and Becky Thatcher Contests. In the past there have also been other sponsored contests.

National Fence Painting Contest

WHO CAN ENTER?
Boys ages 10–13

WHAT IS IT?
Have you heard the story of Tom Sawyer? In Mark Twain's book, Tom Sawyer is a clever boy always coming up with new schemes. Once when his aunt made him paint the white fence outside their house, Tom convinced all his friends that it was a great honor to paint the fence. He got all of them to pay him so that they could paint the fence!

Each year there is a picket-fence painting contest in Hannibal, Missouri, the hometown of Tom Sawyer's creator. To compete, boys have to paint a small section of picket fence with whitewash, a kind of watered-down white paint. Boys from all over the United States can enter, but if you're the state winner in one of the 10 states along the Mississippi River, the Hannibal Jaycees will pay for your transportation and lodging.

The contestants in the National Fence Painting Contest are selected by local contests in their home states. Selection and training of each state's contestant is left to the discretion of that state. The Hannibal Jaycees are glad to assist by supplying promotional material and technical data.

On the day of the contest, fences are set up along the Mississippi River in downtown Hannibal. Each contestant gets his tools of battle—a bucket of modern-day whitewash and a large brush. A signal from the starter is given, and the contestants begin to paint the fences as fast as they can. Heats are run, and the winners of each heat then compete for the championship.

Judges score every contestant in the following three categories: costume (40%); speed (30%); and painting quality (30%).

PRIZES:

Winner: Trophy presented by the governor of Missouri and prizes donated by local merchants

Tomboy Sawyer Contest

WHO CAN ENTER?

Girls ages 9–13

WHAT IS IT?

There are four events that focus on outdoor fun of times past. To compete, the Tomboys are judged as to who can blow the biggest bubble with a wad of bubble gum and who can spit watermelon seeds the farthest. Each contestant is given three tries in each event. Those who win enter a minnow catching and slingshot shooting contest. The girl who does the best in all four of the events is chosen as Tomboy Sawyer.

PRIZES:

Winner and Runner-up: Prizes donated by local merchants
Best Costume: Prizes donated by local merchants

Tom Sawyer and Becky Thatcher Contest

WHO CAN ENTER?

Boys and girls age 13 or in Grade 7 from Hannibal schools only

WHAT IS IT?

If you like to talk to people and are good at remembering things, then this contest is for you. Each year, a Tom and Becky are chosen to represent the city of Hannibal. The winners become ambassadors of good will for the city. Finalists in the contest are taken around the city of Hannibal and shown all the sights that a typical tourist would see. Then they are interviewed by a panel of teachers who decide which candidates will become Becky and Tom for the year. Then Tom and Becky make several appearances throughout the year in parades, travel shows, and state fairs, and they greet the riverboat passengers and visiting dignitaries.

PRIZES:

Winners: Plaques stating thanks for their year as "Ambassadors"

State Fair of Oklahoma

P.O. Box 74943
Oklahoma City, OK 73147

TIME OF YEAR:
September

WHAT IS IT?
The State Fair of Oklahoma is 17 days' worth of exciting competitions, displays, and carnival fun.

Gigantic state fairs are great fun because they're a Disneyland of rides and displays and they also have many events in which kids can compete. Picture several acres covered with buildings filled to the brim with prize animals, crops and food displays, machinery of all kinds, crafts, and much more. Picture the judges walking around looking at the different entries and then awarding you a huge blue ribbon!

The State Fair of Oklahoma has 51 regular competitions available for children 10 and under, 68 for children 11 to 13, and 69 open to 14- and 15-year-olds. The competitions range from cake baking to candle making to crafts such as ceramics, papier-mâché, dough art, needlework, and macrame. Rules for the different competitions vary. In the arts and crafts competitions, for example, exhibitors must be residents of Oklahoma, must mail an entry blank to the Fair by August 15, and the work submitted for judging must be the exhibitor's own and have been finished since October of the previous year.

At the Oklahoma State Fair children also compete in special contests held before an audience. These are the Awesome Sandwich Contest and the Ultimate Bubble Contest.

Awesome Sandwich Contest

WHO CAN ENTER?
Ages 10 and under; Ages 11–13; Ages 14–15

WHAT IS IT?
The taste, appearance, and originality of your greatest sandwich will be judged during the Awesome Sandwich Contest. On the day of

the contest, sandwich ingredients (including bread) and a copy of the recipe must be taken to the Junior Department in the Hobbies, Arts, and Crafts Building at the Fair. Contestants will prepare their sandwiches in front of the audience and judges, and then the tasting will begin. The best-looking, tastiest, and most unusual sandwiches win.

PRIZES:

Best of Show: Medallion
First Prize in each age category: $25
Second Prize in each age category: $15
Third Prize in each age category: $10
Fourth Prize in each age category: $5

The Ultimate Bubble Contest

WHO CAN ENTER?

Ages 7 and under; Ages 8–9; Ages 10–11; Ages 12–13

WHAT IS IT?

Contestants in the Ultimate Bubble Contest check in at the Lattice Stage in the Hobbies, Arts, and Crafts Building on the day of the contest. Bubble gum is provided, and bubbles blown will be measured by the judges, who will name winners in each age category.

PRIZES:

First Prize in each age category: $5 and a medallion
Second–Tenth places in each age category: Ribbons

World Championship Crab Races

Crescent City–Del Norte County Chamber of Commerce
P.O. Box 246
Crescent City, CA 95531

WHO CAN ENTER?

All ages

TIME OF YEAR:

Mid-February

WHAT IS IT?

Entering a crab in a crab race.

It's fun to watch a lot of crazy crabs, including your own, race along a 4-foot track with the help of a trainer just like you. You can also have a good time urging your pet crab to hustle its legs to victory. Several hundred crabs will vie for the World Championship. This event goes all day.

The admission fee is $1, and the racing fee is $2. If you want to rent a crab it will cost $1, but you can bring your own. You can also enjoy a crab meal as you watch the crab races.

PRIZES:

Grand Champion: $100 and a crab trophy
Winner in each category: Crab trophy

(You have to show up to discover what a crab trophy is, but we can tell you that it is described as "Dungeness.")

CHAPTER 6

Creating: Getting Your Name in Print

TIPS ON WRITING

Do you like to write short stories, poems, or plays, or make up jokes and puzzles, or draw pictures or take photographs for other kids? Well, if you do, maybe you'd like to see some of your work in print. It's not at all impossible. There are quite a few children's and family magazines that are looking for material done by children.

The magazines listed below will publish your work if you send them what they want. Some of them will even pay you for it. How much will they pay you? That depends. The prizes or awards vary from magazine to magazine. In many instances the only reward is seeing your name in print and being able to say, "I am a published author." That alone should make you feel fabulous. On the other hand, some magazines pay a fee for published materials, anything from $1 up.

As you will see from reading the following descriptions, many of the magazines sponsor special contests from time to time. Prizes for these contests include T-shirts, trips, savings bonds, cash, and copies of the magazine in which your work appears. If you are interested, go to the library and look through some of these magazines to find out what kind of contests are being sponsored. Then decide which contests, if any, you want to enter. Be sure to check the deadlines. You don't want to send in your good work after the deadline has passed.

Here are some hints to help make writing for magazines a success for you:

- Go through the list of magazines listed below and think about which ones might be the most interesting to you. Your school or town library probably subscribes to most of them. One editor wrote a word of advice to young writers: "Get a library card, borrow books and periodicals, and read, read, read."
- If there is one magazine you really would like to have a copy of to study and you can't find it at your library or on the newsstand, you can send for a sample copy. There are two ways to do this. Check the publisher's address in the front of the magazine, check the price of the magazine, add some postage, and send for a copy. Or you can write to the publisher enclosing a self-addressed postcard and ask how much you will need to send for a sample copy. Very often, in this case, the publisher will send you a free copy.

- If a magazine really interests you, check the description to see if there are writers' guidelines. Send for them. When you write to ask the editors for the guidelines, be sure to include a self-addressed, stamped envelope. Then follow the writers' guidelines carefully.
- As you look through the magazines, also be sure to check for the kinds of materials other kids have had published. Editors don't print materials that don't fit their themes—so be careful your work is the type of material the magazine publishes. Don't send jokes, for example, to a magazine that doesn't publish jokes.
- Check all grammar, punctuation, and spelling in your final copy before sending it in. If at all possible, your final copy should be typed and double-spaced. It also helps if someone reads your copy for you, because others often can pick up mistakes that you don't see. And—try not to cry, cringe, or creep away if you feel that someone is too critical. We know. You worked so hard, but maybe some changes will improve what you have done.
- When you send your work to the magazine, be sure to include a short letter of introduction giving your name, address, age, phone number with the area code, and school year.
- Keep a copy of anything you send, since many magazines don't return materials. And sometimes stuff gets lost.
- Be sure to include a self-addressed, stamped envelope for the return of your material if it is not going to be published. That is the only way you will know if it is not going to be.
- Remember that if your work isn't accepted the first time, you can try again. Submit your material to another magazine as soon as possible. Don't give up too easily. Sometimes it takes many tries before somebody wants to publish your work.
- If you send the same copy out too many times, though, it may start to look dog-eared. Of course you don't want to, but write, type, or draw it over. You do want to see it published, don't you?
- Plan ahead. Magazines usually work about six months ahead, so if you have an idea for a Valentine's Day story, submit it around late August or early September.
- Check to see if you need to send a note from your parent or teacher stating that the work you are submitting is your original work.
- Keep a careful record of what you send out, where you send

it, and when. Ask some adult to help you with this, if you need to.

- Every editor makes changes, and your writing will probably be edited before it is printed. Editors often change things to a style or format that they believe is best for their publication and their readers. Don't be upset by this. It happens. And, hey, at last something with your name on it is right there in that magazine for everyone to see. Congratulations!

Boys' Life

Magazine Division
Boy Scouts of America
P.O. Box 152079
Irving, TX 75015-2079

Boys' Life is the magazine of the Boy Scouts of America. It has several columns where readers can be published, including "Hobby Hows," "Stamps and Coins," and "Think & Grin." Occasionally, there is a special reader's page or a contest. Send a self-addressed, stamped envelope for writers' guidelines.

Capper's

616 Jefferson Street
Topeka, KS 66607

WHO CAN SEND IN MATERIAL?

All ages

Capper's has a special section called "Space Place" where they publish original drawings, photos, poems, stories, puzzles, and jokes by children. *Capper's* awards special T-shirts to kids published in "Space Place." Writers' guidelines are available.

Chickadee

The Young Naturalist Foundation
56 The Esplanade, Suite 306
Toronto, Ontario M5E 1A7
Canada

WHO CAN SEND IN MATERIAL?

Ages 3–9

Chickadee encourages readers to submit drawings on themes announced each month, jokes, riddles, news, and views all year-round. In addition, *Chickadee* holds an annual Cover Contest, announced in October. Rules for the contest are given in the magazine. Send international postal coupons if you want unaccepted material returned. Ask at the post office about this.

Child Life

Children's Better Health Institute
1100 Waterway Boulevard
P.O. Box 567
Indianapolis, IN 46206

WHO CAN SEND IN MATERIAL?

Ages 7–9

Child Life publishes fiction (up to 500 words), poems, and occasionally puzzles, photos, recipes, and artwork submitted by its readers. Material with a health-related theme or idea is preferred. This includes good nutrition, safety, exercise, and proper health habits.

Children's Album

P.O. Box 6086
Concord, CA 94524

WHO CAN SEND IN MATERIAL?

Ages 8–14

Children's Album encourages children to submit poems, stories, and plays (no longer than 1,000 words each). They also accept original color artwork. They will send you writers' guidelines if you mail them a self-addressed, stamped envelope.

Children's Digest

Children's Better Health Institute
1100 Waterway Boulevard
P.O. Box 567
Indianapolis, IN 46206

WHO CAN SEND IN MATERIAL?

Ages 8–10

Children's Digest publishes fiction or nonfiction stories (up to 700 words), original poetry, children's favorite jokes and riddles, and readers' opinions on specific questions. Material with a health-related theme or idea is preferred. This includes good nutrition, safety, exercise, and proper health habits.

Children's Playmate

Children's Better Health Institute
1100 Waterway Boulevard
P.O. Box 567
Indianapolis, IN 46206

WHO CAN SEND IN MATERIAL?

Ages 5–7

Children's Playmate publishes original poetry, original artwork, and interesting jokes and riddles by children. Poetry may or may not rhyme. Material with a health-related theme or idea is preferred. This includes good nutrition, safety, exercise, and proper health habits.

Cobblestone: The History Magazine for Young People

Cobblestone Publishing, Inc.
30 Grove Street
Peterborough, NH 03458

WHO CAN SEND IN MATERIAL?

Ages 5–14

Cobblestone is a monthly American history magazine. Each issue has a theme—biography, historical event, cultural topic, etc. Some recent topics have been Frederick Douglass, Hispanic Americans, People with Disabilities, Environmentalism, The Navajo, and Thomas Jefferson. *Cobblestone* accepts letters, drawings, and short poems for its letters pages. Writers' guidelines are available.

Creative Kids

P.O. Box 6448
Mobile, AL 36660

WHO CAN SEND IN MATERIAL?

Ages 5–18

Creative Kids publishes materials from gifted, creative, and talented children. The magazine includes poetry, stories, music, puzzles, activities, parodies, limericks, plays, cartoons, artwork, photography, material for further discussion, pen pals, and reviews of books and games. For all material you submit, a form must be completed and signed by a parent or teacher stating that the work is original.

    Creative Kids also has three ongoing contests: Goofy Gadgets, Create-a-Game, and the Cover Photo Contest. Winners receive a free subscription. Send a self-addressed, stamped envelope for information on the contests and writers' guidelines.

Creative With Words

P.O. Box 223226
Carmel, CA 93922

WHO CAN SEND IN MATERIAL?

All ages

Creative With Words accepts children's poetry, seasonal and holiday stories and poems, folk tales, and fairy tales. Children's written work should be sent with a letter from a parent or teacher saying that it is original writing. Writers' guidelines are available with a self-addressed, stamped envelope.

Cricket Magazine

P.O. Box 300
Peru, IL 61354

WHO CAN SEND IN MATERIAL?

Up to age 14

Cricket Magazine holds monthly contests for writing, poetry, photography, and/or art on many different themes. Specific rules for each contest appear on the "Cricket League" page of each monthly magazine.

Dolphin Log

The Cousteau Society
8440 Santa Monica Boulevard
Los Angeles, CA 90069

WHO CAN SEND IN MATERIAL?

Ages 7–15

Dolphin Log is The Cousteau Society's bimonthly magazine for kids. Often, readers are invited to send in drawings or stories relating to articles, and some are published. There are also many contests for readers.

Dynamite

730 Broadway
New York, NY 10003

WHO CAN SEND IN MATERIAL?

Age 8 or older

Dynamite is an entertainment magazine with articles about celebrities, stories, jokes, puzzles, and contests. Each issue has a "Bummer" column. A "Bummer" begins with "Don't you hate it when...." Readers are invited to send in their ending to the sentence and are paid $5 if their "Bummer" is published. Contests are announced in the magazine and winners are awarded prizes like cameras, keyboards, and bicycles. Recent contests have asked for photos of readers dressed as their favorite rock stars and of teddy bears dressed up.

Hidden Pictures Magazine

P.O. Box 51480
Boulder, CO 80321-1480

WHO CAN SEND IN MATERIAL?

Ages 6–12

Hidden Pictures Magazine is full of jokes, riddles, games, teasers, tricks, word scrambles, mazes, hidden pictures, and clues. Keep an eye out for upcoming games and contests to play.

Highlights for Children

803 Church Street
Honesdale, PA 18431

WHO CAN SEND IN MATERIAL?

Ages 2–12

Highlights for Children publishes stories, pictures, and poems from readers. This material must be your own work, and you must send with it a note from a parent, guardian, or teacher saying that it is original. *Highlights* also accepts drawings for "Creatures Never Seen," as well as short descriptions of favorite books and easy-to-make recipes. Other writing and drawing topics are announced every few months. See a copy of the magazine for examples. Riddles and jokes are also accepted and do not need to be original or have a parent note with them. Readers' contributions cannot be returned. Writers' guidelines are available.

Can you tell us how you got started in the activity?

. . . .

"I always wrote. Whether it was poetry, stories, or even games to play. I love it. I wrote for my school newspaper and loved journalism, composition class. When I found out about it, I immediately knew I had to enter. My advice to anyone who would like to start in this wonderful activity would be, 'Keep on writing.'"

Kathy Garruba

Humpty Dumpty's Magazine

Children's Better Health Institute
1100 Waterway Boulevard
P.O. Box 567
Indianapolis, IN 46206

WHO CAN SEND IN MATERIAL?

Ages 4–6

Humpty Dumpty's Magazine publishes artwork or pictures that children have drawn or colored. The magazine also publishes children's comments on special issues, along with a photo of the writers.

Jack and Jill

Children's Better Health Institute
1100 Waterway Boulevard
P.O. Box 567
Indianapolis, IN 46206

WHO CAN SEND IN MATERIAL?

Ages 6–8

Jack and Jill publishes contributions in the following categories: interesting letters, jokes and riddles, original stories, book reviews, and articles (not longer than 500 words), original poetry, and artwork. Material with a health-related theme or idea is preferred. This includes good nutrition, safety, exercise, and proper health habits.

Kids' Computer News

St. Hilda's and St. Hugh's School
619 West 114th Street
New York, NY 10025

WHO CAN SEND IN MATERIAL?

Ages 6–15

Kids' Computer News is published for members of Technology Not Tricks, the Computer Club of St. Hilda's and St. Hugh's School in New York City. Kids in other schools can join the club as associate members and then be eligible to receive the newsletter. Each month, the editors look for the best computer programs, reviews, articles, humor, tips, hints, and graphics. The members who submit the best work each month receive six months added to their subscriptions. Writers' guidelines are available.

KIND News

67 Salem Road
East Haddam, CT 06423

WHO CAN SEND IN MATERIAL?

Ages 6–12

KIND News is a monthly newspaper about the importance of kindness to living things and the environment. Two versions are published, one for grades 2–4 and one for grades 5–6. Readers are encouraged to submit letters, news items, and photos. There are also bimonthly contests for readers.

Koala Club News

Zoological Society of San Diego
P.O. Box 551
San Diego, CA 92112

WHO CAN SEND IN MATERIAL?

Ages up to 15

Koala Club News accepts riddles, drawings, letters, and photographs about wild animals from club members. They also have contests. For example, one contest asked members to send in captions for photographs of animals. By subscribing to the magazine you become a member of the Koala Club of the San Diego Zoo and are entitled to visit the zoo or wild animal park. You will need to write to find out how you can become a member.

McGuffey Writer

McGuffey Foundation School
5128 Westgate Drive
Oxford, OH 45056

WHO CAN SEND IN MATERIAL?

Ages 5–17

The *McGuffey Writer* accepts short stories, essays, poems, cartoons, and illustrations in black and white. Items are accepted on the basis of merit, originality, and appropriateness. There are requirements for manuscripts: your name, grade level, school, and address must be on every page; a teacher or parent must sign the first page to verify that the work is original. The editors prefer to see the original copy of your work.

National Geographic WORLD

17th and M Street, NW
Washington, D.C. 20036

WHO CAN SEND IN MATERIAL?

Ages 8–12

National Geographic WORLD sponsors fabulous contests. Over the years, *WORLD* has run contests such as Plant-a-Seed, Save the Animals, Art, Safari, Design-a-T-Shirt, Photography, Make a Super Sandwich, Drawing Grotesques, and Geography Scholarship. To keep track of *WORLD* contests, look in individual issues of the magazine and follow the rules given. If you or a friend have done something very interesting, consider writing about it for the "Kids Did It" section of the magazine.

Odyssey Magazine

Ms. Nancy Mack, Editor
21027 Crossroads Circle
P.O. Box 1612
Milwaukee, WI 53187

WHO CAN SEND IN MATERIAL?

Ages 6–16

Odyssey Magazine conducts monthly contests on various outer space topics. Subjects such as the space shuttle and future vehicles are typical, and sometimes readers are asked to submit puzzles and poetry on similar themes. An annual cover contest accepts drawings about anything concerning outer space. There are three age categories for this contest: Ages 8 and under, Ages 9 to 12, and Ages 13 to 16. There is a monthly section of letters from children concerning their interests in outer space.

OWL

The Young Naturalist Foundation
56 The Esplanade, Suite 506
Toronto, Ontario M5E 1A7
Canada

WHO CAN SEND IN MATERIAL?

Ages 8–14

OWL encourages readers' submissions of drawings, jokes, riddles, news, and views all year-round. In addition, *OWL* holds many contests, including an annual writing contest, poetry contest, cover contest, and an awards program—called the Hoot Club awards—which honors kids who have done something special to help the environment. Rules for the contests are announced in the magazine. Don't forget: You will need to send international postal coupons for the return of unaccepted material.

Skipping Stones

80574 Hazelton Road
Cottage Grove, OR 97424

WHO CAN SEND IN MATERIAL?

All ages; priority given to young writers and artists under 18 years of age. Minorities are especially invited to send submissions.

Skipping Stones publishes original artwork, stories, songs, poems, riddles, and recipes by children of all ages and cultures. The magazine also encourages children to send in writings about their backgrounds, cultures, religions, interests, and experiences. Submissions are welcome in all languages. Writers' and artists' guidelines are available.

Spring Tides

Savannah Country Day Lower School
824 Stillwood Drive
Savannah, GA 31419-2643

WHO CAN SEND IN MATERIAL?

Ages 5–12

Spring Tides is a literary magazine published by the Savannah Country Day School. It encourages students from other schools to submit their work. You can submit stories of up to 1,200 words and poems of up to 20 lines. These stories and poems can be with or without illustrations. Your work needs to be typed. Send your name, address, birth date, grade, school, and school address. You also need to send a statement from your parent or teacher saying your work is original. Include a stamped, self-addressed envelope if you want your material back. If your work is published, you will get a free copy of that issue.

Stone Soup

P.O. Box 83
Santa Cruz, CA 95063

WHO CAN SEND IN MATERIAL?

Ages 6–13

Stone Soup is the nation's oldest literary magazine entirely by children. It is published five times a year and is completely devoted to fiction, poetry, book reviews, and artwork by children. Each issue includes color artwork created by children from around the world, as well as an Activity Guide. Writing and art from children is welcome, especially stories and poems based on real-life experiences and observations. Send a self-addressed, stamped envelope for writers' guidelines.

Wee Wisdom

Unity School of Christianity
Unity Village, MO 64065

WHO CAN SEND IN MATERIAL?

All ages

Wee Wisdom has a special section called the "Writer's Guild" where they publish poems and artwork by children.

Wordworks

The Young Writer's Club
P.O. Box 216
Newburyport, MA 01950

WHO CAN SEND IN MATERIAL?

Ages 8–14

Wordworks publishes poems, short stories, and letters from children who subscribe to the newsletter and become members of The Young Writer's Club. You will need to send a letter of inquiry about what you have to do to become a member.

Young Authors' Magazine Anthology

Theraplan, Inc.
3015 Woodsdale Boulevard
Lincoln, NB 68502

WHO CAN SEND IN MATERIAL?

Ages 5–12

Young Authors' Magazine Anthology is a book for gifted children that publishes both fiction and nonfiction short stories, plays, and poems. Cartoons are also accepted for publication.

youngperson

360-B Greenwich Street
New York, NY 10013

WHO CAN SEND IN MATERIAL?

Ages 8–14

youngperson is a monthly newspaper that has many contests and also accepts letters from children. You will need to look in individual issues for contest rules.

What do you think we should tell other kids about the contest you won?
....

"They should know that, by reading a lot, they can become better writers and have a chance at being published and getting writing awards."

Jonathan Rosenbaum

Dragonfly: East/West Haiku Quarterly

Middlewood Press
P.O. Box 11236
Salt Lake City, UT 84147

WHO CAN SEND IN MATERIAL?

All ages

Haiku are very short three-line poems with 17 or fewer syllables in all. To write good haiku you create exact pictures with words. The things you describe in your poem will speak for themselves, just as an oak tree often stands for strength and long life. These should be quick sketches, not little stories. *Dragonfly* runs regular contests, and rules are published in the magazine. The editor writes: "We are quite interested in publishing good haiku by children. Rather than worry about guidelines, children would do well to read a lot of examples of haiku. They should practice writing short/long/short lines and stick with images they can see, smell, touch, taste, or hear." You will need to study the haiku form before you submit your work. Writers' guidelines and sample copies are available.

Family Computing

730 Broadway
New York, NY 10003

WHO CAN SEND IN MATERIAL?

All ages

Family Computing asks readers to submit essays on how computers are affecting their lives. The editors are also interested in receiving your computer designs, your best computer jokes, and computer game strategies. The magazine pays for contributions accepted and published.

Grit

208 West Third Street
Williamsport, PA 17701

WHO CAN SEND IN MATERIAL?

All ages

Grit is a tabloid-size national weekly that prints stories about individuals and groups who are making an important contribution to their neighbors, community, and/or the American way of life. There's also a kids' page that asks for kids' stories, poems, and drawings. Use a dark, felt-tip pen when you draw. A story should be 100 words or less. If you know of a kid who has an unusual business, hobby, or pet, write to *Grit* to see if they are interested in having you write a story about this person. Poems should be no longer than 12 lines. Enclose a note from your parents or teacher verifying that you didn't trace or copy the material you are sending. Always include your name, age, and the town where you live. No contributions can be acknowledged or returned. Writers' guidelines are available.

What do you think we should tell other kids about the contest you won?
....

"If you have something to write about, just write it."

Jamie DeWitt

Sunshine Magazine

P.O. Box 40
Sunshine Park
Litchfield, IL 62056

WHO CAN SEND IN MATERIAL?

All ages

For "The Voice of Youth" pages, *Sunshine Magazine* accepts short stories and poems that are easy to read, rhythmic, and uplifting. There is a "Pen Pal" page that prints letters from kids who describe their interests and ask other kids to write them. A riddle column prints riddles on seasonal themes. Writers' guidelines are available if you send a self-addressed, stamped envelope.

CREATING FOR NEWSPAPERS

Many newspapers print kids' stories, poems, book reviews, and drawings. Here are some tips on how to figure out if a certain newspaper is a good place to send your work:

- If the paper publishes a kids' page such as *Pennywhistle Press,* or if entries are accepted for a locally written kids' page or column, it's worth calling them or writing to them to find out their rules and requirements.
- See if your newspaper participates in Newspaper in Education Week, which is held every year in February or March.

If your local newspaper has a section that's written by children, please let us know. Remember, we are eager to get this information, as well as information on contests. If your local newspaper doesn't sponsor children's pages or contests, why don't you talk to your teacher or parents and see if something can be done about it? It's possible the editor could be encouraged to add a kids' page. It might be worth a try. You might be one of the first contributors.

Here are some hints to help you get published in a newspaper:

- Go through your newspaper carefully to see if there is a children's page, a kids' column, or announcements about contests for kids. If not, talk to your parents and teachers.
- Alert your parents to watch for occasional contests in the paper if you don't get to read the paper every day.
- If you do send something to a newspaper, you can expect quicker publication than in a magazine. Newspapers are set up to get the news and other stuff to their readers in a short period of time—days or weeks instead of months.
- When you submit any material to a newspaper, be sure to send with it a letter in which you give your name, address, telephone number, and school year.
- Check your work for spelling, punctuation, and any errors in grammar before sending it in. It also helps if someone reads your copy for you, because others often can pick up mistakes that you don't see. Don't be upset if that person is a bit "picky." You did ask for help, didn't you?
- Keep a copy of anything you send, since newspapers usually don't return materials.

- Every editor makes changes in materials submitted, so your writing will probably be edited before it is printed. Expect materials to be cut to fit the space available. Don't fuss. Just be glad your stuff was accepted.

Here is a list of some children's pages and special events in newspapers. We know that this is a very small sample, so we encourage you to check for yourself in your local newspapers.

CHILDREN'S EXPRESS

20 Charles Street
New York, NY 10014

WHO CAN SEND IN MATERIAL?

Reporters: Ages 8–13; **Assistant Editors:** Ages 14–18

TIME OF YEAR:

Any time

WHAT IS IT?

CHILDREN'S EXPRESS is a private, nonprofit news service reported by children who are 13 and under. The reporters work in teams, led by assistant editors who are 14 to 18 years old, to put out the nationally syndicated *CHILDREN'S EXPRESS* column twice a month. The column reports on serious, real world issues that affect children.

CHILDREN'S EXPRESS has seven news bureaus in the United States and overseas. The column has appeared in many major American newspapers, including *The New York Times, Chicago Sun-Times, Cleveland Plain Dealer, Miami Herald,* and *San Francisco Examiner.* The Japanese *CHILDREN'S EXPRESS* column has a regular circulation of 9.4 million. Bureaus are located in Melbourne, Australia; Wellington, New Zealand; the San Francisco Bay Area; Boston, Massachusetts; Newark, New Jersey; New York City; and Tokyo, Japan.

CHILDREN'S EXPRESS has developed training in oral journalism, which enables children from a wide variety of backgrounds to participate in its activities. Columns consist of interviews with commentary by the young reporters or a round-table dialogue between reporters and other children the same age. Their work is supported by teen editors and a small adult staff.

The Houston Chronicle

Educational Services Department
801 Texas Avenue
Houston, TX 77002

The *Houston Chronicle* conducts the Student Essay Contest and the View and Review Contest each year.

Student Essay Contest

WHO CAN ENTER?
Middle School: Grades 6–8; **High School:** Grades 9–12

TIME OF YEAR:
March

WHAT IS IT?
The Student Essay Contest is an opportunity for students to be rewarded for good writing and good citizenship. They are asked to write about Houston and to explain why they think it's a desirable place in which to live.

PRIZES:
Winners in each division: Wristwatch. Winners and their parents will also be invited to a special awards ceremony and to watch a Houston Astros baseball game from the *Houston Chronicle*'s skybox.

View and Review Contest

WHO CAN ENTER?
Category One: Ages 7–9; **Category Two:** Ages 10–13

TIME OF YEAR:
September

WHAT IS IT?
Students are asked to attend a local play and then to write a drama critique of the production.

Iowa City Press-Citizen
Newspaper in Education Week Contests

319 East Washington Street
Iowa City, IA 52240

WHO CAN ENTER?

Grades 1–3; Grades 4–6; Grades 7–9; Grades 10–12

TIME OF YEAR:

March

WHAT ARE THEY?

The *Iowa City Press-Citizen* conducts yearly contests during Newspaper in Education Week that might be good to enter if you live in the Iowa City area. You can write to the paper to find out about this year's contests. For example, the paper has conducted a Creative Classified Contest.

Creative Classified Contest

Contestants were asked to choose a classified ad from the *Press-Citizen* and to use that ad as a basis for a creative story. Each story had to be 200 words or less, typewritten or neatly written by hand, and had to have the ad on which it was based attached. Each entry had to include the author's name, address, phone, age, school, grade, and teacher's name. Winning entries were published in a special section of the *Press-Citizen*.

PRIZES:

First Place in each division: $25
Second Place in each division: $15
Third Place in each division: $10

The Morning Call
Newspaper in Education Week Contests

Public Relations Contests
P.O. Box 1260
Sixth and Linden Streets
Allentown, PA 18105

TIME OF YEAR:

February or March

WHAT ARE THEY?

To celebrate Newspaper in Education Week every year, *The Morning Call* conducts great contests. If you live in the Allentown, Pennsylvania, area, you might want to check the paper to see what contests it is holding this year. In 1986, the paper held a Creature Feature Contest, a Cosmic Collage Contest, and a Lively Limerick Contest. Each of these contests had a category for special education students. For children with special needs, teachers discussed which of the three contests might be best for them to enter.

On the back of each contest entry students must write their name, home address and telephone number, age, grade, teacher's name, school, and the school's address and telephone number. All entries without this information are disqualified. No student can submit more than one entry per contest.

Creature Feature Contest

WHO CAN ENTER?

Kindergarten–Grade 4

WHAT IS IT?

For the Creature Feature Contest, children cut out objects from advertisements, photographs, and other illustrations in *The Morning Call.* They use them to create a creature from outer space and to name it! Paste your creature on paper 8½ by 11 inches and write the creature's name at the top.

Cosmic Collage Contest

WHO CAN ENTER?

Grades 5–8

WHAT IS IT?

For the Cosmic Collage Contest, you imagine that a spaceship has landed on Earth, and that you have been chosen to help these aliens learn about Earth. Using items and information from *The Morning Call,* children create collages to express what life on Earth is like today. Entries should be no larger than 18 by 24 inches.

Lively Limerick Contest

WHO CAN ENTER?

Grades 9–12

WHAT IS IT?

For the Lively Limerick Contest, children write a limerick on a space-related topic or story that appeared in *The Morning Call*. The limericks must be attached to the newspaper articles on which they were based. Entries are to be typed or written legibly on paper 8½ by 11 inches.

State Times and Morning Advocate

Educational Department
525 Lafayette Street
Baton Rouge, LA 70821

TIME OF YEAR:

All year

WHAT IS IT?

The *State Times and Morning Advocate* publishes a syndicated children's page called "Bubble Gum Rapper." The newspaper also conducts several contests each year. They are the Current Events Rally, the Design–an-Ad Contest, and the Favorite Foods Contest.

Bubble Gum Rapper

WHO CAN SEND IN MATERIAL?

Ages 5 and over

TIME OF YEAR:

All year

WHAT IS IT?

"Bubble Gum Rapper" is a children's page which appears weekly in many newspapers. Each week the page focuses on a theme and is designed to entertain kids with word and number games, word searches, picture completions, coloring activities, jokes, and fun facts. Kids can submit original drawings, puzzles, games, and jokes.

Current Events Rally

WHO CAN ENTER?

Elementary School: Grades 5 and 6
Middle School: Grades 7 and 8
High School: Grades 9 and 10

TIME OF YEAR:

January

WHAT IS IT?

For the Current Events Rally you submit scrapbook collections of newspaper articles supporting your point of view on a topic such as "The Environment." Your notebook will be judged on neatness, how well the selection of articles supports the position you have taken on the topic, and the originality of the cover design. Students are chosen by their teachers to participate in this contest, then they begin to keep a scrapbook. Each student whose scrapbook is judged best in a school competition gets to attend the Current Events Rally. At the rally, contestants write essays on the current topic, complete a multiple-choice test made up of questions about the topic, and then participate in an oral team presentation in which they respond as a team to a question about a preselected topic.

PRIZES:

Elementary and Middle School
First and Second prizes: Trophy and cash

High School
First Prize: Two-week, all-expense-paid trip to Europe
Second Prize: Trophy and cash

Design-an-Ad Contest

WHO CAN ENTER?
Grades 4–12

TIME OF YEAR:
March

WHAT IS IT?

For the Design-an-Ad Contest, children register with the paper and are assigned a business for which they design an ad. Individual retail advertisers who have bought space in the special supplement do the judging. They select the ads that they like the best and then the ads are published in the "It's Good News in Education" supplement. Ads are judged on creativity, originality, and neatness. Ads must be submitted on an official entry form and be for local businesses, so you will have to live in the Baton Rouge area.

PRIZES:
Certificates of Merit for all winners

Favorite Foods Contest

WHO CAN ENTER?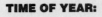
Kindergarten–Grade 3

TIME OF YEAR:
March

WHAT IS IT?
For the Favorite Foods Contest, children are asked to draw pictures of their favorite food and then to describe in writing how they think it should be prepared. If the student doesn't yet know how to write, an adult may write down the child's words. Entries are judged by *State Times and Morning Advocate* food editors on creativity, originality, organization, and neatness. The winning entries will be published in "It's Good News in Education," a supplement to the newspaper.

PRIZES:
Certificates of Merit for all winners

The Times

500 Perry Street
P.O. Box 847
Trenton, NJ 08605

The *Times* prints four special features to which kids in the Trenton area can submit material. They are Create-an-Ad, Funtimes, *New Jersey and Youth,* and the *Literature Times.*

Create-an-Ad Contest

WHO CAN ENTER?
Grades 1–6

TIME OF YEAR:
Newspaper in Education Week, February or March

WHAT IS IT?
For the Create-an-Ad Contest, kids draw and write advertising copy for local businesses. They have to draw and explain why the business is a great one and one that people should use. Judges are the owners of the businesses for which the ads are created. The top three ads for each business are chosen to be published in a special section of the *Times.* The winning ads are also shown at a Newspaper in Education Week display at the local shopping mall.

Funtimes

WHO CAN SEND IN MATERIAL?
Kindergarten–Grade 9

TIME OF YEAR:
Any time

WHAT IS IT?
"Funtimes" is a locally written kids' page published on Sunday. It accepts letters, short pieces of creative writing, word finds, drawings, and poems from kids for publication.

New Jersey and Youth

WHO CAN SEND IN MATERIAL?
Kindergarten–Grade 12

TIME OF YEAR:
May

WHAT IS IT?

New Jersey and Youth is a student publication sponsored by the New Jersey Reading Association and the *Times*. Kids submit letters, ads, real estate listings for homes of famous people, drawings, sports items, and cartoons for publication.

How did you feel when you won?
....

"It was a very special feeling knowing I had reached a goal I had worked so hard for. It was all worth it and I couldn't have been happier."

Alan Francis

Literature Times

WHO CAN SEND IN MATERIAL?
Grades 1–6

TIME OF YEAR:
June

WHAT IS IT?

The *Literature Times* is a joint publication of the Hamilton Township (New Jersey) School District and the *Times* Newspaper in Education Program. Any child in the school district can submit letters, book reviews, drawings, word searches, sports stories, clever advertisements, cartoons, maps, and local news.

Young American

P.O. Box 12409
Portland, OR 97212

WHO CAN SEND IN MATERIAL?

Ages 5 and over

TIME OF YEAR:

Any time

WHAT IS IT?

Young American is a newspaper supplement published two times a month. It is published to give children a sense of being a part of today's important events, and the editors are particularly interested in stories about newsworthy kids. They are also very eager to publish children's articles about current events, sports, science, computers, and entertainment, and will also accept drawings, fiction, and poetry. Children are asked to state their age with each submission. Send a self-addressed, stamped envelope for writers' guidelines.

PUBLISHING A BOOK, SHORT STORY, PLAY, OR ESSAY

Writing a book is a big project for anyone. It takes time and it takes energy. Often the material has to be written over and over again until it's just right. However, there are kids who have successfully published books. If you are interested in seeing your name in print, it might be a good idea to ask an adult to help you. You may need someone to stand by and give you encouragement if you get discouraged and want to give up.

To get off to a good start, get the rules for publishing the book from the groups listed below. Read them carefully. Then have an adult sit down with you and make sure that you understand how you're going to do the work. Get the materials you need and decide if there are goals you need to set for yourself. For example, how much work do you need to do each week to make the deadline? Do you have to set up a place in the house to do your work?

Here is a list of some writing contests.

Adlyn M. Keffer Memorial Short Story Writing Contest

National Story League
NSL Contest Chair
561 Old Orchard Lane
Camp Hill, PA 17011

WHO CAN ENTER?

Junior: Grades 4–12
Adult: After high school

TIME OF YEAR:

Stories must be submitted between January 1 and April 1 annually.

WHAT IS IT?

Do you have an idea for a short story you would like to write? Your story can be funny or sad. It can be a mystery, an adventure story, a horror story, or even a science fiction story. As an author you can decide who the people are in your story, what happens to them, and how the story ends. The possibilities for stories are endless. You're the boss. Let your imagination be your guide.

This short story contest is open to all members of the National Story League and others interested in short story writing. You must submit three copies of your story. Your story must be typed and double-spaced on one side of a page only. The story must not exceed 2,000 words, and the number of words in your story should be placed in the right-hand corner of your title page. You may submit only one story, and it must be original. No stories will be returned. If you are not a member of the Story League, you will need to enclose a check for $5. Or, for $15, your whole class at school can all send in entries together.

Stories must be suitable for oral telling. A good way to practice is to tell your story to your English class or to your parents and friends. This will help you write your story in a more exciting way. Create a story by starting with a problem and follow through to a solution.

Your story will be judged on eight qualities; each quality is worth a certain number of points. The story writer with the most points wins. Here are the eight most important qualities. Make sure that you keep all of them in mind when you write your story.

1. Title (10 points): The title is an important part of the story. Is it interesting, suitable to the story, and not too long?
2. Beginning (10 points): Does the opening sentence or paragraph make you want to read the story?
3. Ending (10 points): Is the ending definite, pointed, and clear? Does it bring the story to a climax?
4. Plot (15 points): Is the plot simple and yet interesting, with only one story in it?
5. Characters (10 points): Are the characters real and vivid? Can you hear them in action in your imagination?
6. Use of expressive language (10 points)
7. Tellability (15 points): Because the stories will be used mainly for oral telling, it must be a tellable story. Would it need to be cut or lengthened?
8. Originality and creativity (20 points): Does the story remind you of something you have read or heard before?

If your story is a winning entry it will be published in *Story Art Magazine*. After your story is published, the rights to submit it again for publication are returned to you one year after your manuscript was received.

PRIZES:

First Place: $20 and story published in *Story Art Magazine*
Second Place: $15 and story published in *Story Art Magazine*
Third Place: $10 and story published in *Story Art Magazine*
Three Honorable Mentions: Letter of praise and a copy of the *Story Art Magazine* in which your story is published

WHAT ARE MY CHANCES?

In 1990, 70 people entered and there were 7 winners.

Publish-A-Book Contest

Publish-A-Book Contest
Raintree Publishers
310 West Wisconsin Avenue
Milwaukee, WI 53203

WHO CAN ENTER?

Grades 2–3
Grades 4–6

TIME OF YEAR:

January 31 deadline

WHAT IS IT?

The theme of the Publish-A-Book Contest changes each year. Most recent topics have included adventure, heritage, and your imagination. The winning story is published as a book and sold as part of the publisher's regular list. Your teacher or librarian must sponsor your writing. To date, approximately 20,000 students have entered the first three Publish-A-Book contests.

PRIZES:

First Prize: $500, your book published for sale, and copies of the book
Twenty Second Place winners: $25 and 10 books

Annual National PTA Reflections Program—Literature Category

National PTA
Reflections Program
700 North Rush Street
Chicago, IL 60611-2571

WHO CAN ENTER?

Students must be in a school that has a PTA or PTSA. Kids can enter at these levels:

Primary: Kindergarten–Grade 3
Intermediate: Grades 4–6
Junior High School: Grades 7–9
Senior High School: Grades 10–12

TIME OF YEAR:

State contests: January through March
National contests: April

WHAT IS IT?

Writing is a great way to express your thoughts and feelings. And the best thing about writing is that you can do it almost anywhere—in your room, in a car, on a train, in a tree, in your doctor's waiting room, or wherever you happen to be. All you need is a pen or pencil, some paper, your imagination, and perhaps a clipboard.

Writing can take any form—a poem, a story, or even words written to go with music. Ask your school's PTA about participating in Reflections. Talk to your parents or a teacher to make certain that what you write qualifies according to the National PTA's rules.

Here are the rules:

1. If desired, single-sheet literary entries may be mounted on lightweight material, but the overall dimensions of a mounted entry may not exceed 11 inches by 14 inches. The use of any material heavier than poster paper or lightweight cardboard is discouraged. Mounting is not required, and entries are judged on literary content, not artwork.

2. Multiple-page entries may be attached to folders, put together in booklet form, or clipped together. Entries in any form may be no larger than 11 inches by 14 inches.
3. Entries may be written by hand or typed, but in either case the work must be done by the student. Exception: If a student is handicapped, someone else may write or type the student's original work.
4. A photocopy of the original entry may be entered for judging and the original copy retained by the student. Copies are given the same consideration by the judges as originals. Entries will not be returned.
5. All entries must be the original work of the entrant, done without any help from parents, friends, relatives, or teachers.
6. All entries must be accompanied by an application, signed by the entrant's parent, verifying that all work was done without help. A signed permission release must accompany the entry, too.
7. You may enter more than one poem or short story, but you may not enter anything done by more than one person.

Each year the Reflections program has a special theme. All entries must relate to and express the year's special theme. Each year the theme changes. If your writing does not express or relate to the special theme, then you must be sure to use this theme in the title or subtitle of your work. The 1990–1991 theme was "If I Had a Wish." The 1991–1992 theme is "Exploring New Beginnings."

PRIZES:

First Place winners: $300

Second Place winners: $200

Third Place winners: $100

Outstanding Interpretation winner: A trip to the National PTA convention with an adult guardian, a $250 scholarship, and a gold-plated Reflections medallion

Honorable Mentions: World Book Annual or Children's Annual

Winners are announced at the National PTA Convention, in the PTA magazine, and in newsletters. For more information, write to the National PTA.

National Written and Illustrated by...
Awards Contest for Students

Landmark Editions, Inc.
P.O. Box 4469
Kansas City, MO 64127

WHO CAN ENTER?

Category A: 6–9 years old
Category B: 10–13 years old
Category C: 14–19 years old

TIME OF YEAR:

May 1 deadline

WHAT IS IT?

Imagine a book written and illustrated by you winning the National Written and Illustrated by...Awards Contest! You and your parent would get an all-expenses-paid trip to Kansas City where you'd meet with editors, artists, and layout people to work on the final draft of your book. It would be a week of one-on-one interaction between you and these professionals to get your book ready for publication. And then when your book is actually published, you would receive royalties from the sales of the book. The winner and four runners-up in each of the three age categories will receive college scholarships from the R. D. and Joan Dale Hubbard Foundation.

To prepare your book for entry in the contest, you will have to follow guidelines that are available from Landmark Editions, Inc. All entries must be submitted with the approval of your teacher or librarian and a parent. There are specific rules about the number of pages in your book (at least 16 pages but not more than 24 pages) and the number of illustrations (one picture for every two-page spread). Your drawings may be made with any medium as long as they are two-dimensional and flat to the surface of the paper. There are clear guidelines about the type of paper, the binding, and the cover. All books will be reviewed by a panel composed of professional writers, illustrators, teachers, and school librarians. They will be judged on originality and the writing and illustrating skills displayed.

Each student whose book is selected for publication will be offered a complete publishing contract. To ensure that students benefit from the proceeds, royalties from the sale of their books will be placed in an individual trust fund set up for each student by the parents or legal guardians at a bank of their choice.

To obtain a copy of the official contest rules, guidelines, and entry forms, please send a self-addressed, stamped business-size envelope to Landmark Editions, Inc. at the above address.

Young Writer's Contest

Young Writer's Contest Foundation
P.O. Box 6092
McLean, VA 22106

WHO CAN ENTER?

Grades 1–8

TIME OF YEAR:

Fall (October/November)

WHAT IS IT?

The Young Writer's Contest Foundation has established this contest to encourage kids' writing and to give them a chance to get their work published in an anthology of stories.

To enter the contest, you will need to have your teacher sign an official entry form stating that the writing you submit is your own original work. Send a self-addressed, stamped business envelope with your request for the entry form. In addition, your school will have to pay a $15 entry fee for you and the other kids who enter. The maximum number of entries per school is 12.

Other rules for the contest follow:

1. Entries should consist of poetry and short stories or essays of no more that 500 words, written in the English language, typed or legibly printed in black ink on one side of each page only. Acceptable paper size: No smaller than 8 inches by 10 inches and no larger than 8½ inches by 11 inches. Each entry must be the original and current work of the student alone and must not have been previously published.

2. Each entry must be accompanied by a registration form that provides complete identifying data.
3. Entries will be judged on the basis of grade level. The specific judging criteria will be grammar (spelling and punctuation, verb tenses, etc.) and content (creativity, originality, clarity, organization of ideas). It Is, of course, natural to write on seasonal topics, but do consider a variety of subjects.
4. Each packet of 12 entries (or less) must be accompanied by one check for $15 (registration fee), plus one stamped, self-addressed, business-size envelope (used to provide a list of the winners when they are announced). Due to the large volume of entries, receipt cannot be acknowledged unless a self-addressed, stamped postcard is included.
5. Entries must be postmarked by November 30 and be received within 14 days of that date or they will not be included in the competition.
6. Winners will be announced in the first week of March. Winning entries will appear in a specially published volume, *Rainbow Collection* anthology, which will be available in May.
7. All entries become the property of the Young Writer's Contest Foundation and cannot be returned, so please keep a copy for your records.
8. All participants (students and schools) receive certification.

Child's Play Touring Theatre

2650 West Belden, Suite 201
Chicago, IL 60647

WHO CAN SEND IN MATERIAL?

Grades Kindergarten–8

TIME OF YEAR:

Whenever your school, local museum, arts council, park district, shopping mall, bookstore, or library invites Child's Play to perform in your area.

WHAT IS IT?

Child's Play Touring Theatre performs plays, songs, and dances based on stories and poems written by children. When a school, museum, arts council, park district, shopping mall, bookstore, theatre, or library wants to hold a contest for children in their area, they ask children to submit their work. Then they invite Child's Play to judge the poems and stories and to create a production based on them. When the Child's Play troupe gives their performance, the children can see the characters and ideas from their stories and poems come to life on the stage!

Child's Play performances are interactive—that means that the actors use the children in their audiences as participants in their productions. When kids walk into a performance, the Child's Play troupe is already on stage juggling, dancing, and performing mime routines. Within minutes the professional actors get students from the audience to join them in their antics. As soon as children are settled into their seats, the scheduled performance begins. The troupe usually performs a number of works, all written by children. Some of the plays have been written by children in the audience, who are viewing the world premiere of their creative work.

If a group in your community sponsors a Child's Play performance, there are guidelines for the adults in charge and also for you, the writer, to follow when you submit your work.

1. You can write about anything. It can be funny or serious.
2. You can write a story or a poem or an essay or a play.

3. Stories and poems can be as long as you want.
4. All of the words must be created by children. Don't copy from a book, a TV show, a movie, or your neighbor.
5. You can work with one or more friends, even your entire class.
6. Please send drawings and artwork if you'd like.
7. Please try to write neatly.
8. Remember to print your name, teacher's name, and school.

If you want more information about how to bring Child's Play to your community, write to the address above.

PRIZES:

Seeing your story, poem, play, or essay performed and receiving a certificate from Child's Play.

WHAT ARE MY CHANCES?

Last year, Child's Play performed 528 of the 4,111 submissions they received.

Henny Penny Playwriting Contest

Children's Radio Theatre
1314 14th Street NW
Washington, D.C. 20005

WHAT IS IT?

In the past, winning playwrights have joined the team at Children's Radio Theatre for a weekend of activities in their honor. Winning plays were also produced on the air.

At the time of publication of this book, the Children's Radio Theatre was not certain as to whether funding will be available for the Henny Penny Playwriting Contest. Contact them if writing plays is one of your favorite activities.

Can you tell us how you got started in the activity?
....

"From as far back as I can remember, I have liked to read. After reading certain series (the Hardy Boys, for example), I would pretend to be an author and write in a style similar to what I had just read. I've just always liked to express myself through words (and pictures and music)."

Jonathan A. Rosenbaum

CHAPTER 7

Belonging to Groups and Entering Their Contests

JOINING A CLUB

Belonging to a club can be lots of fun. As a member of a group, you can learn new skills and share good times with other kids your age all at the same time. Joining a group is a good way to meet kids who are interested in the same things you're interested in. In fact, if you've just moved to a new neighborhood, joining a club is one of the best ways of making new friends.

Entering contests is really not a good reason for joining a group. On the other hand, if your club happens to run a special program or sponsor a contest (and most clubs will have at least one or two in a year), why not take part in the activity? It may give you a chance to experiment with something new and exciting, and many times you can earn badges, patches, certificates, and other awards for participating.

In this chapter, we describe only a small number of award programs and contests, and they are all sponsored by national youth organizations. If you belong to one of these groups, great! If you don't—there are hundreds of similar programs run by local youth groups. It won't take much to find one! Or you might think about joining 4-H or the Boys Club or Girls Club.

4-H

4-H is a program for children ages 7–19 that helps them learn useful skills and to become good citizens. The name stands for head, heart, hands, and health. When 4-H first began, about 60 years ago, it was set up mainly for kids who lived in farming communities, but this is no longer true. The 4-H club is great for kids who live in cities and suburban areas, too.

Here are some of the ways you can be involved in 4-H:

- 4-H Clubs: This is a year-round program for a group of kids who meet once or twice a month to plan their own special program under the leadership of a teenager or adult. 4-H club members can choose from about 50 different kinds of projects. For example, a group of kids who love to cook might form a 4-H cooking group.
- Special Interest Groups: These groups work on a project for part of the year. This project does not have to be one of the special 4-H programs. For example, some kids might get together during the summer and decide the greatest thing for them to do would be to form a group where all they do is go swimming, dancing, and horseback riding and play tennis.
- School Programs: Your school might have a special 4-H program, such as a safety program, or your teacher might do some 4-H activities in the classroom.
- Family Clubs: If you live too far away from a town with a 4-H club, your family can form a 4-H club and your parents become the 4-H leaders.
- On Your Own: You can plan and direct your own special program with the help of an adult or parent. For example, if you like to wander in the fields and meadows and identify plants, you might like to keep a record of your findings as part of your horticulture project.

Kids 7–9 are usually called Clover or Junior Members. These younger members work on short-term projects and do not participate in the 4-H project contests or shows. Those in the 10–19 age group are called 4-H Club Members. They can enroll in a project by keeping a 4-H record sheet on an activity such as bread making, seed identification, or veterinary science. For example, if you choose to do bread making, your 4-H record sheet would include all the important facts you learned while baking bread, the skills you gained, the things you enjoyed most about the project, and "your best picture" of a loaf of bread you baked.

Entering Your Project in a 4-H Fair

Many 4-H agents wrote us and told us that their 4-H programs do not encourage competition among kids between the ages of 6 and 12. Instead, the program tries to help participants to be successful to the best of their abilities.

Still, kids between the ages of 10 and 19 can compete at local, county, and state fairs. If you have worked on a project and completed a 4-H record sheet, you might want to enter your project in the local or county 4-H fair. If you do a bread baking project, for example, it will be judged with other kids' who are also baking bread in the towns near where you live. If your project is chosen as one of the winners at the county fair, it can then be entered in the state fair. And, when you are older, you can also compete at the national 4-H fair. For many events you could receive participation ribbons, trophies, and money.

The projects available for kids will vary from state to state. After you get involved, you will find out if you can participate in these projects at the local, county, and state levels. Here are some typical 4-H projects:

Animal Science
Bait Casting
Beef Show
Bee Keeping
Better Citizens/
  Better Communities Activity
Bicycle Activity
Bread Making
Clothing
Craft Activity
Crops Science
Dairy Cattle Judging
Dairy Show
Dancing
Dog Care, Training, and Shows
Ecology
Entomology (insects)

Fashions
Flower Arranging
Foods and Nutrition
Forestry
Gardening
Goat Show
Health Activity
Home Environment Activity
Horse Shows
Horticulture
Instrumental Activity – Classical and Nonclassical
Junior Eggs Program
Livestock Judging
Market Hog Program
Meat Judging and Identification

Photography
Plant and Soil Science
Poultry Expo
Public Speaking
Rabbit Show
Safety Activity
Seed Identification
Sheep Show
Small Engines
Steer Feeding
Swine Show
Talent Show
Turkey Show
Veterinary Science Activity
Weed Identification
Wheels and Motors
Wood Science

Becoming a 4-H Member

If you are interested in joining 4-H, look for a 4-H flyer at school, in the library, or in the newspaper. Also, you might visit an open house at a Cooperative Extension Service where your 4-H state leader has an office. Remember, 4-H programs are available both in the city and country.

FOR INFORMATION ON LOCAL 4-H PROGRAMS, WRITE:

4-H Youth Programs
U.S. Dept. of Agriculture Extension Service
Washington, DC 20252

Boys Clubs of America (BCA)

771 First Avenue
New York, NY 10017

Boys Clubs serve children and youths ages 6–18. The club has centers in many cities and offers programs after school, Saturdays, and summers. In some cities, Boys Clubs also include girls. Some of the many interesting activities offered are computers, fine arts, photography, team sports, fitness, and social events.

Member of the Boys Clubs can enter these two yearly contests—the Young Artists Program in Fine Arts and the Young Artists Program in Photography.

Boys Clubs of America Young Artists Program—Fine Arts Exhibit Program

WHO CAN ENTER?

Any Boys Club member who has been enrolled in his club for at least three months. Members belonging less than three months may exhibit at the local level but not at the regional or national level. There are five age levels:

Class I: Ages 9 and under
Class II: Ages 10–11
Class III: Ages 12–13
Class IV: Ages 14–15
Class V: Ages 16–18

TIME OF YEAR:

Local exhibit: January
National exhibit: Spring

WHAT IS IT?

Boys Club members create artwork and then display it in an exhibit.

Creating a work of art takes lots of imagination. Displaying your finished work in an art exhibit can sometimes be the best reward—everyone feels like a winner when they can take parents, friends, and grandparents to view the exhibit. It's equally exciting when people stop to look at your work and exclaim "Wow, that's neat!" or "That's a great job!" Try eavesdropping by your work to hear what people say about it!

Crafts and industrial arts will not be accepted for this exhibit. Tracings, follow-the-dots or numbers, or other artwork for which a ready-made pattern is used will not be accepted, either. You may submit your artwork in more than one of the following categories:

- Drawing: Drawings include artwork created with pencil, charcoal, markers, and pen and ink
- Crayon: Artwork created with wax-type crayons
- Pastel: Artwork created with chalklike pastels or oil-based pastels
- Watercolor: Artwork created with pan type, tube, or tempera paints
- Oil or acrylic: Artwork created with oil-based or acrylic paints on any surface
- Printmaking: Artwork that is an impression of a composition produced on a master surface, such as woodcut, linoleum, engraving, etching, or serigraph
- Mixed media: A combination of any of the above media produced on a two-dimensional surface
- Collage or montage: Artwork created by pasting together, on a flat surface, materials such as newspaper, wallpaper, printed text and illustrations, photographs, or cloth
- Sculpture: A three-dimensional work of art, either relief or in the round

On the local level, a club may determine how many pieces of work a member may submit in each category. The maximum number of works a local club may enter in a regional exhibit is one work in each exhibit category from each class. Other rules include:

1. All work must have been created within one year of the exhibit.
2. Frames should not be used on any pictures except mounted oils.
3. Oils mounted on canvas, whether commercially or self-mounted, should be framed with 1-inch-by-¼-inch lattice strips.

 What do you think we should tell other kids about the contest you won?
. . . .

"It takes a lot of work but when you win it feels like you have really accomplished something."

John Schade

4. Watercolors, pastels, sketches, and prints should be matted and backed heavily.
5. Pastels should be sprayed with a fixative before being matted.
6. No work, including matting, may exceed the size of 30 inches by 40 inches.
7. You don't have to create your artwork at your Boys Club, but then your teacher or parent must sign your entry form to verify that the work is your own.
8. You must fill out an information card for each work submitted and attach it to the back of your work with tape or rubber cement.
9. An individual club may participate in only one local exhibit.
10. If your work is not selected for further judging, it will be returned to you by mail.

Each member must fill out an official entry form to enter. By January 1, your club must apply to conduct a sanctioned local exhibit. Any regular or associate member Boys Club, whether or not it has an established art program, may make an application to conduct a local exhibit. Also, a group of neighboring clubs may jointly conduct a local exhibit. Local exhibits should be held from November to January. The judges select a number of works from local exhibitions that will be exhibited at the regional level. Regional exhibits are held from February to March. If your work is chosen by the judges again at the regional level, your artwork will be submitted for national judging at the Boys Clubs of America Annual National Conference in the spring. The judges at all levels will include art experts, such as local artists, curators of local galleries or museums, university art teachers, and art editors of local newspapers. Judging will be based on the age of the exhibitor and skill in the particular medium. Judging at the local and regional levels is left to the discretion of local clubs. On the national level, Boys Clubs of America will have works examined by a panel of judges who will select artwork to be shown at the National Conference. The panel will also make recommendations regarding possible candidates for the Epstein Fine Arts Fund Scholarship in Art.

PRIZES:

All national participants: Certificate
All national participants whose work is selected for exhibition at the National Conference: Presentation folder that contains certificate and photograph of artwork

Boys Clubs of America Young Artists Program—Photography

WHO CAN ENTER?

Any Boys Club member in these age groups who has been enrolled for at least three months is eligible to enter the competition. Your Boys Club must be a regular or an associate member of the Boys Clubs of America.

There are three age levels:
Class I: Age 10 or under
Class II: Ages 11–13
Class III: Ages 14–18

TIME OF YEAR:

February

WHAT IS IT?

Boys Club members take photographs and enter them in this contest.

Do you know your photography personality? Some photographers like to take pictures of nature, others like to take pictures of people, and still others prefer animals as subjects. If you find that you are taking pictures of only one kind of subject, experiment by taking photographs of something you might usually pass by.

The rules for the contest are:

1. Photos may be black and white or color. Photographs may be taken with any camera and with any kind of film.
2. Photographs may be any size up to 8 inches by 10 inches.
3. Photographs may be cropped, leaving any portion desired, but they cannot be mounted. Any size color transparency is eligible.
4. Your photographs may be of any subject. All photography entries must have been taken during the 12-month period before the February deadline.
5. You must include the following information, typed on a separate piece of paper and taped to the back of the photograph: Your name, age, name of your club, title of your picture, type of camera used.
6. Negatives do not have to accompany photographs, but be sure that you have them on hand in case you become a

winner. All winners will be asked to send negatives of winning prints immediately after judging.

7. You may submit as many photographs as you want for local club screening, but you may submit only three photographs for national judging.

8. A local club may submit up to 10 photographs in each age group.

9. All material entered for national judging becomes the property of Boys Clubs of America. You must give permission for its use in reports of the contest, news release displays, and BCA publications. Release information from persons photographed may be required.

10. Pictures having already won an award, including Special Merit Awards, are not eligible.

11. When you send pictures by mail, be sure to protect them by using stiff cardboard.

Each Boys Club must fill out an official entry form and submit it with the photographs taken by club members. If there are lots of photography entries from members in your club, your club may decide to hold a local contest in order to decide which photographs will be submitted for national judging. The Boys Clubs of America will choose a panel of judges that will include professional photographers and photography experts. Photographs will be judged on the basis of general interest, originality, composition, and quality.

PRIZES:

First Prize in each age category: $100 Eastman Kodak gift certificate and a Certificate of Merit

Club of each First Prize winner: $100 and an enlargement of winning photograph

Second Prize in each age category: $75 Eastman Kodak gift certificate and a Certificate of Merit

Club of each Second Prize winner: Enlargement of winning photograph

Third Prize in each age category: $50 Eastman Kodak gift certificate and a Certificate of Merit

Club of each Third Prize winner: Enlargement of winning photograph

Special Merit Award in each age category: $25 Eastman Kodak gift certificate and a Certificate of Merit

Club of each Merit Award winner: Enlargement of winning photograph

Kodak Club Award for Local Club Competition winners: Medal

All participants: Certificates

Boy Scouts of America

1325 Walnut Hill Lane
Irving, TX 75038

Joining a Boy Scout group is an exciting way to make new friends and to learn how to work with others. As a Boy Scout, you can work on any of 100 Merit Badge programs, which help you build skills. Some of the most popular Merit Badge programs are archery, basketry, camping, canoeing, and citizenship. Working with computers, cooking, studying environmental science, fingerprinting, first aid, fishing, forestry, hiking, home repairs, horsemanship, Native American lore, leather work, studying mammals, metalwork, personal fitness, pioneering, public speaking, rowing, small-boat sailing, sports, swimming, wilderness survival, and wood carving are other favorite activities.

The programs in Scouting are Tiger Cubs (1st grade), Wolf Cub Scouts (2nd grade), Bear Cub Scouts (3rd grade), and Webelos (4th and 5th grade). Boy Scouts are for ages 11–17. There are several different age levels in scouting: Tiger Cubs (age 7), Cub Scouts (ages 8–10), Boy Scouts (ages 11–17), Varsity Scouts (ages 14–17), and Explorer Scouts (ages 15–20). You and your friends can join when you are in the first grade and progress in Scouting for years. Some of the contests held at the local council level for Cub Scouts are:

- Cubmobile Derby
- Kite Flying Contest
- Photo Scholarship Awards Contest
- Pinewood Derby
- Pumpkin Carving Contest

Entering a Scouting Contest

By being a Scout you will learn of the many contests held in your local Scout unit. However, there is one national contest for all members.

Boy Scouts of America Photo Scholarship Awards

WHO CAN ENTER?

Any registered Scout may participate in this contest. There are three divisions: Cub Scouts, Boy Scouts/Varsity Scouts, and Explorer Scouts.

TIME OF YEAR:

October

WHAT IS IT?

Scouts enter their best photographs in the contest.

In photography the subject you choose, the way you frame it in your camera lens, and the lighting all contribute to your pictures. The people who see them will be excited, amused, amazed, or pleased based on how you compose all the elements.

The rules are:

1. A maximum of three photos per Scout may be submitted.
2. Photographs may be black and white or color.
3. Photographs may be any size up to 8 inches by 10 inches, but 5 inches by 7 inches is preferred.
4. All photographs must be taken after October 1 for the following year.
5. All photographs must be the original work of a Scout.
6. All photographs must be accompanied by a completed official entry form.
7. Youth members who have won a Grand Award in the past will not be eligible for the competition until they become eligible to enter in the next Boy Scout division.
8. The photographer of each prize-winning photograph will be required to supply the negative or transparency of the photograph to the Boy Scouts of America upon request.
9. All rights to winning photographs become the property of the Boy Scouts of America. Release information from persons photographed is required. Every effort will be made to return nonwinning photographs to contestants who provide self-addressed, stamped envelopes.

The Boy Scouts of America appoints photographic experts as judges. All entries are judged on the basis of originality, impact, composition, and good camera technique. It is possible for a photograph to win two awards. For example, you could win both the Grand Award and the Chief Scout Executive's Award.

PRIZES:

Grand Award for winning photograph in each division: $1,000 U.S. savings bond

Three First Awards for next three best photographs in each division: $100 Kodak gift certificates

Chief Scout Executive's Award for best photograph: portraying Cub Scouting, Boy Scouting, Varsity Scouting, or Exploring: $500 U.S. savings bond

Honor Awards for entries demonstrating photographic excellence or creative applications: $25 Kodak gift certificates

FOR MORE INFORMATION, WRITE TO:

Boy Scouts of America Photo Scholarship Awards
1325 Walnut Hill Lane
Irving, TX 75062

Camp Fire, Inc.

4601 Madison Avenue
Kansas City, MO 64112

Camp Fire members include kids up to age 21. About 35% of the members are boys. Camp Fire reaches young people in four major ways: clubs, camping, self-reliance courses, and child care and child development courses. Members may participate in one or several of these programs.

About 60% of Camp Fire's members are in the club program. Clubs meet regularly, usually once a week, with an adult leader. At Camp Fire resident and day camps, members enjoy crafts, cooking out, hiking, singing, and playing games with friends. Camp Fire also has outdoor activities such as sleep-outs, archery, canoeing, horseback riding, and environmental projects. Over 75,000 members each year attend Camp Fire self-reliance courses such as "I'm Safe and Sure," "I'm Peer-Proof," and "I Can Do It!"

As a member of Camp Fire, you can join the annual Art Competition.

Art Competition

WHO CAN ENTER?

You must be a currently registered member of Camp Fire.

TIME OF YEAR:

Spring

WHAT IS IT?

Camp Fire members create a work of art in a medium assigned by Camp Fire, Inc.

Even the best artists in the world sometimes can't come up with ideas for their art. If this happens to you, it may help if you learn more about your medium. Going to visit a gallery or art studio or going to the library and taking out some books may give you a push in the right direction. After this you may even want to try out some far out and wild ideas! Remember, you can change, redo, and add details to your artwork as you go along. It often helps to experiment.

Every year Camp Fire chooses a particular medium that you must use to create your artwork. The chosen medium is based on an established six-year cycle, which includes painting, fibers, printmaking, photography, clay, and an open medium.

You may create your artwork at home, school, church, camp, in a club meeting, or in an art class. You can create your artwork alone or with a group of friends. You may also enter artwork you have entered in other competitions, as long as it was created with the year's assigned medium. Craft kits, patterns, or copies of already designed pieces are not acceptable in this competition.

To enter, you submit your artwork with an entry form to the council in which you are registered. Number of entries, judging date, and entry forms are determined by your local council. Check with your Camp Fire leader to find out the exact deadline and rules of your local art competition.

Art entries will be judged on:

- Originality of design or the creative expression of the artist's overall idea
- Appropriateness of materials and techniques used to carry out the creative expression and the theme
- Overall composition—line, color, balance, design
- Skill in executing the selected techniques

Judging will be done by a panel of art experts selected by your local council. Judges might include art teachers, professional artists, and gallery curators.

PRIZES:

Prizes vary. Most local councils will present special merit awards to the top three entries and about 12 honorable mentions.

Girls Clubs of America

30 East 33rd Street
New York, NY 10016

The Girls Clubs of America serves girls between the ages of 6 and 18. There are 240 Girls Clubs centers across the United States offering programs after school, Saturdays, and summers.

Every year the Girls Clubs of America sponsors a National Awards Program. There are two types of contests in the National Awards Program: individual contests and club contests. You can enter more than one of the contests for individual members if you have more than one interest. Remember, you'll need the help of your parents or club leader to complete your entry.

Some people like to work on a project by themselves. Kids tell us some of the reasons they like to work alone: they can dream up exciting ideas by themselves, decide how their contest entry should look, and get all the fame and glory if they win. If these things are true about you, too, look to see if there is a contest for you.

Donna Brace Ogilvie Creative Writing Awards for Poetry

WHO CAN ENTER?

Any Girls Club member who is between the ages of 6 and 18 as of January 1 may participate. There are four age levels:

Group A: Ages 6–8
Group B: Ages 9–11
Group C: Ages 12–13
Group D: Ages 14–18

TIME OF YEAR:

January and February

WHAT IS IT?

Girls express their ideas and feelings by writing poetry.

Have you ever thought you'd like to be a poet? Do ideas for poems come to you everywhere—on the street, in a restaurant, at the movies? Well, if they do, just write some of these ideas down before they get away from you. A single thought can be the basis of a good poem. You can work on it later when you have the time.

The rules are:

1. Entries are limited to two poems per member at the local level; only one poem per age category should be submitted for regional judging.
2. Poems may be in a traditional form, such as a limerick or sonnet, or in free verse. Poems can be rhymed or unrhymed.
3. Entries must be at least four lines long; there is no maximum line limit.
4. Entries must be the work of one person and not the result of group effort.
5. Entries must be accompanied by an official entry form from GCA's National Awards Packet.

The first judging of your poetry is at the local club level. If your entry wins at the local level, your club sends it to the regional competition by the second week of January. By the first week of February, regional judges select two regional winners in each age category. If your entry wins at the regional level, it is sent to the national competition. National judging is done by a panel of professional writers and editors, and poems are judged on creativity and expressiveness.

PRIZES:

National Award for winners in Groups A–C: Book

National Award for winner in Group D: $500 scholarship and an all-expenses-paid trip to the Girls Clubs of America National Conference

Local winner in each age category: Certificate of Achievement

Regional winner in each age category: Book

Eastman Kodak Photography Contest

WHO CAN ENTER?

Any Girls Club member between the ages of 6 and 18 as of January 1 is eligible to participate.

Group A: Ages 6–13

Group B: Ages 14–18

TIME OF YEAR:

January

WHAT IS IT?

Girls Club members take photographs to enter in a contest.

Is photography your hobby? Well, no matter what—whether you're taking pictures just for fun or because you hope to become a professional some day—taking a winning picture can be quite a challenge. What if you don't win anything? Don't be discouraged! You can always start a photography collection to hang on your bedroom wall. And there are always other contests coming along.

Your photograph can be of any subject. If your photograph is a picture of a Girls Club or a club activity, or if it was taken using creative techniques, you may be eligible for a special award.

The rules for the contest are:

1. Each Girls Club may submit two photographs to the national competition for each age category.
2. Entries must have been taken after January 1. For example, for the 1992 contest, all photography entries must have been taken after January 1, 1991.
3. Entries may be black and white or color; print sizes may range from 3½ inches by 3½ inches to 8 inches by 10 inches. Slides and instant prints are acceptable. Photos must be unmounted.
4. Entries must be accompanied by a camera original (a negative, transparency, or instant print).
5. To prepare photographs for entry, you must put a label on the back of the photo with your name, age, name of your Girls Club, state, and region. Mail the photograph between two pieces of stiff cardboard.
6. Entries become the property of Girls Clubs of America, which

has the right to use award-winning photographs for purposes of exhibition, audiovisual production, advertising, and publication. Entries not selected for awards will be returned if you send a self-addressed envelope with the correct postage.

7. Entries must be accompanied by a signed photo release from each person in the photo. Release forms must also be signed by a parent or guardian.

8. Photographs must be accompanied by an official entry form.

If your entry wins at the local level, your club sends it to the national competition by the second week of January. National decisions are made by a panel of professional photographers. All photographs are judged on subject matter, originality, visual impact, composition, and technique.

PRIZES:

First Prize: $100 Kodak gift certificate. The first-place winner in Group B will also receive an all-expenses-paid trip to GCA's National Conference.

Second Prize: $75 Kodak gift certificate

Third Prize: $50 Kodak gift certificate

Award of Excellence for best photograph of a Girls Clubs Activity: $100 Kodak gift certificate

Special Merit Award for best photograph demonstrating excellence or unique applications: $5 check

All National Finalists: Certificates

A Girls Club member who wins a prize receives an award certificate and a mounted enlargement of her winning photograph. Also, her club will win an award. The awards are:

Club of each First Prize winner in each age category: $200 Kodak gift certificate

Clubs of winners in each age category: Mounted print enlargements of award-winning photographs

Girl Scouts of the United States of America

830 Third Avenue
New York, NY 10022

The age levels in Girl Scouting are Daisy Girl Scouts for ages 5 and 6 (or Kindergarten–Grade 1), Brownie Girl Scouts for ages 6–8 (Grades 1–3), Junior Girl Scouts for ages 8–11 (Grades 3–6), Cadette Girl Scouts for ages 11–14 (Grades 6–9), and Senior Girl Scouts for ages 14–17 (Grades 9–12). Girl Scout activities help you learn about science, art, and some things about the out-of-doors, and to work easily with people. As your skills grow you will gain self-confidence to help you now and in the future.

Girl Scouts does not place great emphasis on contests or competitions but prefers to give recognition to worthwhile projects that are normally part of Girl Scouting. You can also enter the Keep America Beautiful Week and Youth For America Programs with your Girl Scout troop.

Keep America Beautiful Week Awards

WHO CAN ENTER?

Any group of registered Girl Scouts that runs a Keep America Beautiful (KAB) program throughout the year

TIME OF YEAR:

June

WHAT IS IT?

Girl Scout groups and troops participate in activities that improve their communities and increase other people's awareness about the use of our environment.

Does your Girl Scout troop or group have a great program working to improve something in your community? Maybe you've helped plant greenery in the town square. Does your hard work show both physical improvement in the community and an effort to change attitudes toward the handling of waste and/or the conservation of natural resources? If so, you can report on your project to the organization, Keep America Beautiful, and be eligible for an award. Your program must also have been part of the Keep America Beautiful programs during KAB Week.

If your group's picture has been in the papers or on TV, it will improve your chances of getting an award for the project. And if your idea is really unusual, or can be done easily by other groups, it will receive extra consideration from the judges.

The rules are:

1. Each entry must include a one-page typed summary of the project objectives, the results of the project, and how the project met criteria set by Keep America Beautiful.
2. Entries must be accompanied by photos or slides and no more than 10 pages of information (press clippings, promotional materials, and pamphlets) fastened to 8½-by-11-inch paper and bound in a notebook.
3. Entries will not be returned unless return postage is included.

PRIZES:

Keep America Beautiful National Awards: Engraved "Shadow Box" Awards

All participating groups: Keep America Beautiful Week Certificates of Merit

Colgate's "Youth for America" Awards

WHO CAN ENTER?

Any group of Girl Scouts involved in a community project. Also open to Boy Scouts, Cub Scouts, and other groups.

TIME OF YEAR:

Programs run throughout the year; reports due March 15

WHAT IS IT?

Girl Scout groups that have done community service projects submit reports and win cash prizes.

Colgate-Palmolive's "Youth For America" campaign is offered to many national youth organizations. Groups plan projects to improve their communities, submit reports, and then are eligible for cash prizes. In the past, kids have thought up great projects, ranging from anti-drug abuse programs and after-school homework centers to starting town libraries and restoring historic landmarks. Bonus points are given in the judging for each time a project is reported in newspapers, on TV and radio, and if a mayor proclaims a "Youth For America" week or month. Over the years, the "Youth For America" program has contributed over $4 million to national youth organizations.

In 1987, judges for the contest were Sally Struthers, best known for her role as Gloria in TV's "All in the Family," Phylicia Rashad, Bill Cosby's wife on "The Cosby Show," and Abigail Van Buren, famous for her "Dear Abby" advice column in newspapers throughout the United States.

PRIZES:

National winner bonus prize: $1,000
Local prizes: $100 to $1,000

Young Astronaut Program

Young Astronaut Council
1211 Connecticut Avenue, NW
Washington, DC 20036
Membership information: Jennifer Rae, 1-800-426-4234

WHAT IS IT?

Space has no boundaries and neither do your fantasies about it. Enjoy the excitement of planning for the future by imagining what the future will be like. No doubt by the time you are finished with your education, many people may be living on space stations. You might even be one of them. Well, the Young Astronaut Program will help you imagine what it would be like.

The Young Astronaut Program is for elementary and junior high school students. As a member of a chapter, you can join in exciting activities and receive interesting information on aerospace communications, nonpowered flights, aerospace and the environment, and space and exploration. Some activities include joining a space watch, learning facts about the planets and stars, field trips to space installations and high-tech facilities, joining in national contests, and receiving monthly newsletters.

The Young Astronaut Program was started by President Reagan who, in 1984, said, "I commend the Young Astronaut Program and believe it will help our country achieve even greater heights."

The Young Astronaut Program helps you to understand and plan for the exciting world of the future through many activities, including several different kinds of contests. Over the past several years the following contests have been sponsored: Space Bill of Rights, Young Astronaut Space Olympiad, Young Astronaut National Language Arts, Young Astronaut National Arts/Essay, and Design a Learning Center. We are describing them to give you an understanding of what they were like.

Space Bill of Rights Contest

This contest challenged Young Astronauts to draft a Space Bill of Rights for the citizens living in settlements on Mars in the 21st century. The citizens call their Martian home Terra-Novum, or New Earth. For this contest, each interested chapter conducted its own contest and selected one winner. These "chapter winner" entries were then judged at Young Astronaut Headquarters.

Young Astronaut Space Olympiad Contest

Some people believe that even in space, people will still love sports. Just as there is an Olympic Games on Earth, there may be a Space Olympiad. For the first Space Olympiad Contest, Young Astronaut members were asked to think of an idea for a team sport like soccer or baseball, or an individual sport like javelin or cycling. They were then asked to invent an "out-of-the-world" sport that would be played in an "out-of-the-world" place.

Young Astronaut National Language Arts Competitions

For "The View Out the Window" competition, Young Astronauts were asked to imagine looking out of a window of a space station in 1992 and to write about what they would see: the earth, shuttles, other astronauts. Each Young Astronaut was then to describe the scene in 150 words or less.

Young Astronaut National Arts/Essay Competitions

For the "Letter to a Young Cosmonaut" competition, Young Astronauts were asked to write a letter. They had to describe the United States space program, the possibility of future cooperation between the United States and the Soviet Union in space, and their experiences as Young Astronauts. They could describe their activities, field trips taken, and projects.

Design a Learning Center Competition

Young Astronauts were given a design problem for this competition. "The year is 2055. Several large stations and bases are scattered from Earth orbit to the moon. Several thousand families live in habitats all over cislunar space (the region between Earth and the moon). It has been decided that students from the families working on these bases should have a space learning center. For some of the students, it will mean boarding at the school and flying home for vacations. Others will be close enough to go to the learning center on a daily basis." This contest asked Young Astronaut chapters to work together and submit a group plan for the space learning center.

CONTESTS ESPECIALLY FOR
BOYS CLUB OR GIRLS CLUB LEADERS

In the section that follows, we describe some contests for leaders of Boys Clubs and Girls Clubs. Quite often, leaders are involved in very creative work, but don't take the time to tell others about their efforts. This is where you come in. If you are a member of the Girls Club or the Boys Club, you could read about these contests and tell your leader about them. These are contests that your leader must enter, although the contests all have to do with projects that the kids are doing.

Boys Clubs of America Honor Awards for Program Excellence

Boys Clubs of America
771 First Avenue
New York, NY 10017

ELIGIBILITY:

A Boys Club leader or volunteer must belong to an active club to enter this contest.

TIME OF YEAR:

February

WHAT IS IT?

Boys Club leaders write about a program in their club that they think is terrific.

Some Boys Club programs are so exciting and so much fun that the kids who belong to them can hardly wait until after school to take part in them. If this feeling is familiar to you, you might want to encourage your leader to write about your Boys Club program. By asking your leader to write about something that makes you feel proud, you can share your enthusiasm and inspire others to join the Boys Clubs.

Your Boys Club program must fall into one of seven core area categories. The categories are:

1. Citizenship and Leadership Development: group clubs, special interest groups, community service projects, junior leaders, Keystone and Torch Clubs, and programs that promote international understanding
2. Personal Development Services: youth employment, education for parenthood, computer training, counseling, and prevention of alcohol and drug use
3. Social Recreation: coed activities, hobby groups, game room activities, dances, and movies

4. Outdoor/Environmental Education: camping, conservation trips, nature study, gardening, and community beautification
5. Health and Physical Education: health, gymnastics, fitness clubs, and team sports
6. Cultural Enrichment: performing arts, journalism, photography, library activities, and fine arts
7. Membership Outreach: mainstreaming programs and outreach initiatives

The rules for the contest are:
1. Complete an official entry form.
2. An individual program cannot be submitted in more than one category, but a club may submit several programs for the same category. Nonwinning entries from other years may also be submitted if the program still exists.
3. Programs in the planning stage or those not operating before September 1 of the current year are not eligible. Program entries that duplicate winners from the last five years or Boys Club pilot programs are also ineligible.

All entries are judged on:
- Creative and imaginative thought and planning
- Members' involvement in planning and implementation
- The extent to which the program has a positive impact on the club and/or community
- How easily the program can be copied by other clubs
- How well the program uses local resources
- The program's ability to meet the needs of its members and the community

PRIZES:

National Honor Awards: Commemorative plaques
National Merit Awards: Commemorative plaques

An Honor Award and two Merit Awards are presented in each of the seven categories.

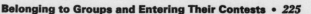

American Association of Retired Persons (AARP) Intergenerational Program Awards

Girls Clubs of America
30 East 33rd Street
New York, NY 10016

ELIGIBILITY:
A Girls Club in good standing with GCA dues and reports up to date

TIME OF YEAR:
January

WHAT IS IT?
Club leaders write descriptions of programming that includes older people.

Having a relationship with an older person is like having a special grandparent for a friend. Many older people enjoy the same activities you do and many enjoy having kids around. Doing things with older people can be a lot of fun. You can learn from them, and they can learn from you.

There are two program categories to which your club leader can submit an entry:
1. Involvement of Older Volunteers: Programs that develop volunteer or staff opportunities for older persons by integrating them into local Girls Clubs.
2. Intergenerational Programs: Programs specifically designed to encourage the old and the young to share experiences.

The rules are:
1. The program must have been completed sometime during the current year.
2. Clubs may submit as many entries as they wish.
3. Entries must be original, but certain models are acceptable.
4. Entries must be typed on an official entry form.

Judging is coordinated by the American Association of Retired Persons and is conducted by specialists in intergenerational programming on the following criteria:

- Program's effectiveness in developing long-term relationships and understandings between old and young people
- Program's ability to involve old and young people in activities with shared purposes and to promote understanding of the aging process
- Program's impact on the girls' development
- Involvement of the girls in planning and implementing the program
- Number of members served
- Uniqueness of the program
- Interagency cooperation the program has started
- Program's effect on the club and community

The Girl's Club of Delaware won for their tutoring program called "Project Pride," in which older people helped teen parents work on G.E.D. degrees and served as role models.

PRIZES:

First Prize: $500 grants to the winning club in each category
Winning club in each program category: Award Certificate

Awards for Fundraising Activities

Girls Clubs of America
30 East 33rd Street
New York, NY 10016

ELIGIBILITY:

A Girls Club in good standing with dues and reports up to date

TIME OF YEAR:

January

WHAT IS IT?

Club leaders write about a successful fundraising activity at their club.

Has your club completed an activity that was fun and raised a lot of money? It might have been a street fair, garage sale, plant sale, or whatever.

There are three categories in which your club may submit an entry:

- Annual Support Campaigns: Activities that may include membership drives and other direct fundraising efforts with individuals, corporations, and foundations.
- Capital or Endowment Drives: Activities that may include raising money for constructing new buildings or fixing old ones, for buying club vehicles, and for other expenses that are not part of the operating budget.
- Support for Core Program: Activities that raise money for specific Girls Club Core Programs.

The rules are:

1. The event must have been completed sometime during the current year.
2. Clubs may submit as many entries as they wish.
3. Bingo is not an acceptable fundraising activity.
4. Entries must be typed and sent in with a completed form.

Judging is conducted by a panel of fundraising experts. All entries will be judged on the amount raised, the size of the club, the resources available in the community, the cost effectiveness of the activity, and the number of people involved.

PRIZES:

Awards are given in three categories.

National Award: Plaque

First Place Award for club staff or volunteers: Certificate

First Place Award for one club in each category: Certificate

Eastman Kodak Photography Program Grant Awards

Girls Clubs of America
30 East 33rd Street
New York, NY 10016

ELIGIBILITY:

A Girls Club with a photography program or one in development. The club must be in good standing with dues and reports up to date.

TIME OF YEAR:

January

WHAT IS IT?

Club leaders describe their photography program or propose an idea for one. They describe how a photography gift certificate could help their club's program.

Although your leader doesn't have to send in pictures for this contest, everyone in the club will surely be taking lots of pictures if there is a great photography program.

The rules are:
1. The club's plan must show how it was created or expanded.
2. A club may submit only one plan.
3. Entries must be typed on an official entry form.

Judging will be done by a panel consisting of staff from Eastman Kodak Company and a nonparticipating local Girls Club. Judging of all photography plans will be based on the following issues:

- The photography program plan for the club, including ideas for cooperating with local Eastman Kodak dealers
- The club's plan to develop or expand a photography program and the extent to which the program will serve the club and the community

PRIZES:

Several national awards: $500 gift certificates from Eastman Kodak

Girls Clubs of America Expansion Awards

Girls Clubs of America
30 East 33rd Street
New York, NY 10016

ELIGIBILITY:

A Girls Club in good standing, with dues and reports up to date

TIME OF YEAR:

January

WHAT IS IT?

Girls Club leaders write about how they have expanded an existing program in their club or how they have increased Club membership.

Have you liked being a Girls Club member and have you shared your excitement and enthusiasm with others? Has your club been successful in adding members? If these things are true, your leader should enter this awards program and tell the judges how your club has spread Girls Clubs fun!

There are two categories to which your club leader can submit an entry:

1. Club Membership Increases: Activities resulting in new members (over 20%) in the club.
2. Programs for New Populations: Expansion campaigns that provide services to a previously unserved group, such as teens or young mothers.

The rules are:

1. The program must have been completed sometime during the current year.
2. Clubs may submit as many entries as they wish.
3. The expansion activity summary must be typed on an official entry form.

Judging will be conducted by organizational development experts from other agencies, based on the following criteria:

- Program's ability to meet its goals

- Program's ability to involve the community to help add more members to the club
- Characteristics that make the program unique

PRIZES:

National awards: Plaques
Staff who develop programs: Award certificates

Girls Clubs of America Outstanding Program Awards

Girls Clubs of America
30 East 33rd Street
New York, NY 10016

ELIGIBILITY:

A Girls Club in good standing, with dues and reports up to date

TIME OF YEAR:

January

WHAT IS IT?

Girls Club leaders write about a program in their club that they think is terrific.

Do you have a program in your club that you think is fun and has helped you learn something new and exciting? If so, why don't you encourage your leader to write about it and enter it in the Outstanding Program Awards contest?

There are seven program categories to which your club may submit an entry:

- Career and Life Planning
- Health and Sexuality
- Leadership and Community Action
- Sports and Adventure
- Self-Reliance and Life Skills
- Culture and Heritage
- Miscellaneous

The rules are:

1. The program must have been completed sometime during the current year.
2. Clubs may enter as many entries as they wish, but may not resubmit entries that have won before.
3. Entries must be original.
4. Entries are not eligible if they are programs being developed with special funding from Girls Clubs of America.
5. Entries must be typed on the official entry form.

Judging will be conducted by a panel of youth program specialists and will be based on the following criteria:

- Program's ability to meet its goals
- Ways the program encouraged members to develop their skills
- Extent to which the members were involved in program planning
- Number of members served
- Uniqueness of the program
- Extent to which the program encouraged members to cooperate
- Ways the program influenced the club and the broader community

PRIZES:

National awards in each program category: Plaques

National awards for staff persons who developed the winning program: Award certificates and $100

McCall's Sewing Program Awards

Girls Clubs of America
30 East 33rd Street
New York, NY 10016

ELIGIBILITY:

A Girls Club in good standing, with dues and reports up to date

TIME OF YEAR:

January

WHAT IS IT?

Club leaders write about a sewing program that teaches clothing construction and that they think is outstanding.

Doing a sewing project as a group can be fun. Together you can come up with many ideas that you wouldn't be able to think of alone. Maybe your club has sewn a gorgeous ball gown or maybe your club chose to sew a farmer's outfit. If you've loved sewing at your club, you can encourage your leader to enter this program.

The rules are:

1. Clubs may not resubmit a winning entry, but are eligible to enter descriptions of other sewing programs. For example, if your club won a suit contest last year, you cannot enter a description of your suit sewing program, but you can submit a description of your dress sewing program.
2. You must have sewn your project sometime during the current year.
3. Clothes designed must be original.
4. The program description must be typed on an official entry form.

To enter, your club leader must mail a description of your sewing program directly to the Girls Clubs of America by certified mail. National judging is done by the McCall Pattern Company and sewing specialists. Descriptions of sewing programs are judged on the following criteria:

- Overall program
- Number of members in the program
- Teaching techniques of the program and its emphasis on sewing as a lifelong skill

PRIZES:

Four club awards (granted according to size of annual operating budget): Sewing machines
Participating clubs: One-year subscriptions to McCall's Pattern Magazine

CHAPTER 8

Running Your Own Contests and Publishing a Newspaper

Having a Contest for Your Friends

We know there were a number of contests we wrote up in this book that you liked. We also know that it's impossible for you to get to many of them just because of the sheer distance. So don't despair! Instead, consider running your favorite contest in this book at your school, after-school program, club, YMCA, playground, summer camp, or community center. Contests are also fun at parties.

Make sure that the contest you pick really interests you, so it will be more fun to stick with it when you have problems. Go through the book again and decide on the contest or contests that you think would be the most fun to run for your friends. If you want to try to run your contest like the organization did, go ahead. However, if you want to modify it, be clear about what you changed and tell everyone who is involved. If there are parts of two different contests you think would make a great combination if they were put together, try to do it. Whether you modify or combine parts of a contest, be sure to include the changes in all of your written material. Most likely your prizes will be different.

Designing a Contest

It could be even more exciting for you to dream up an all-new contest. If you want to try this, it's best to begin with something you're already interested in and that you know a little bit about. If you need some ideas, look at the list "Yes, No, and Maybe" again. Then take your interest in dogs, cats, birds, trees, computers, machines, art, dance, music, comics, baseball cards, or fabrics and brainstorm with other people about how you can create your contest. Here are some ways that you can gather information about the contest you are designing:

- Read all about the topic. This will help you make the contest as interesting as possible.
- Visit any places that might be connected to your contest. For example, if you are planning a dog beauty contest, you might go visit a kennel, a veterinarian, a dog trainer, or dog obedience classes.
- Talk to people who are interested in the subject. If you like to knit, talk to someone who teaches knitting; if you're planning to run a cartoon contest, talk to editors, illustrators, gag writers, and cartoonists.
- Write letters to experts to get information. You can also use the addresses in this book to write to specific people and groups. No question is too silly. It is possible that you'll get the best response if you write a specific person, telling them what you're interested in and asking your questions as clearly as possible.
- New experiences can help you look at a problem differently. If you are going to have a kite-flying contest, you might want to try to fly a kite from the seashore, a tall hill, or a field. This information helps you pull together the rules for your contest.
- Find a person you trust and can turn to when you get stuck and frustrated. Sometimes it helps to solve a problem when you have someone to talk and brainstorm with. Sometimes you even solve your own problems by talking about them out loud.
- Learn a skill to help you if you need it. Maybe it is typing, writing, using a dictionary, putting on makeup, or decorating cakes.
- Make sure that the contest that you design and submit is original.

After you've had time to think about what interests you, go ahead and try to create your contest. To do this, think about:

- The name of your contest. A good name can grab the attention of a lot of people.
- Ages of kids who can enter—eligibility. Some activities are better for a certain age group. Assess how hard your contest is. Then decide on the age group for which your contest would be the most fun. Or you might prefer activities that appeal to all ages, like running, art, writing, or dance.
- Time of year. Think about what time of year, month, or even day would be good for your contest. Sometimes a weekend is better because kids usually don't have too much homework. In the summer, many kids go away to camp or on vacation, so recruiting people in the summer might be harder.
- Rules of the contest. Try to think of all the rules you will need to help make the contest fair. Rules also help judges decide which entries are the winners.
- Judging and the judges. Consider picking a variety of people to be your judges. Choose experts on your topic such as teachers or instructors, musicians or artists. You'll probably want some kid judges, too.
- Prizes. Think about what kinds of prizes you would like to receive if you were a winner. Your prizes don't have to be fancy. For example, you might have one prize be a batch of homemade chocolate chip cookies. Most kids we know love chocolate chip cookies! See if you and others can persuade some local merchants to contribute some of their products for prizes, and talk to your folks about their ideas. For example, maybe a local bowling alley would give a gift certificate for free bowling time.
- Money. You need to know how much money it will cost you for materials for your contest, fliers, prizes, etc. Some ideas may seem great until you find out that they cost a lot. But don't give up—you may be able to find someone to donate the money for it.
- Location. Decide where are you going to hold your contest. If you are going to use a school yard or public park, you may need to contact someone for permission to use it.
- Help. Can you run this contest alone, or will you need some volunteers to help you? If you belong to a group—a 4-H club or Camp Fire group—you could turn this into a group project.
- Trial run. Did you try out your contest? What did the kids think of it? The true test of a good contest is if kids like it. By

trying out your contest on other kids, you soon learn what rules or directions are not clear, what "wrinkles" in the contest you need to iron out, and the ways you can improve it.

- Publicity. Some of the ways you might advertise your contest to other kids is to:

1. Make a flier and decorate it in a catchy way. Be sure to include all the information about the contest, including where kids can find out more about it. Put the fliers up on bulletin boards around town.
2. Talk to your folks and see what ways they think you might be able to publicize it.
3. Ask your teacher if you can publicize your contest by decorating a bulletin board in your school with your announcement.
4. Kick off your contest with a special assembly. For example, if your contest was a "Name As Many Insects As You Can" contest, your kick-off might involve a talk by a local wildlife instructor about insects, along with an explanation of your contest rules.
5. Have a ribbon-cutting ceremony to kick off the start of your contest.

We are sure that you can design a super and original contest. To see if other kids think the same, try your contest out at school, camp, your after-school program, or with a group of kids in your neighborhood. After you've tried it, change the things that didn't work.

Publishing Your Own Newspaper

If you are serious about getting your work published you might like this idea. Most people think only of sending their work away to newspapers and magazines, hoping it will be accepted and printed. Why not publish your own newspaper? You could work it out with some other children in your school, neighborhood, or after-school program. Start with just one issue, and if it works out well and was fun to do, you could think about doing it again.

Groups of children who have done this have the best success when they keep the format rather simple and inviting. For example, if you can use a computer to produce the newsletter, it will make the entire production process much easier. Your newspaper might include stories about other children (for example, a story about kids who collect baseball cards), poems, information on current events, cartoons, jokes and riddles, and crossword puzzles. Have the entire publication be the work of children. You need to decide how long your newspaper will be, what you want to print in it, who your audience is, and how many copies to print up. If you're keeping it very small, you could do all the work yourself. If you get fancy, you're probably going to need help. Then you can divide up the work—one person could be in charge of art, another in charge of typing, another in charge of circulation.

Children who have been involved in such ventures have reported that it is necessary to have an adult or two available to help. It's possible that a local merchant might assist with the funds for printing, and advertising is another way of getting money to pay for paper and printing costs.

If you do create such a newspaper, please send us a copy. In return, we'll put you in touch with other kids involved in the same venture.

Have a great time!

Appendix

What's Fun? What's Fabulous?

This chart has questions for you to answer about what you think you'd really enjoy doing and would do the best. Go ahead and answer these questions. As you answer them, remember we suggest that you enter only those contests that are really of interest to you. Also, your answers to these questions will help you to think about the type of contests that you would find the most interesting to plan and run for other kids.

1. If you could do anything you wanted out of school, what would you do? Describe it.
2. What activity in the whole world would you most like to do?
3. What is your favorite thing to do?
4. What is your least favorite thing to do?
5. When you are not in school, what are the things that your friends do that you wish you could do?
6. What are you good at?
7. What do you think you are horrible at?
8. What do you wish you were better at?
9. What do you wish you could do that you don't know how to do?
10. What do you love to do at school?
11. What do you hate to do at school?
12. What do you do in school that you would like to do out of school?
13. What do you like to do around the house?
14. What do you hate to do around the house?
15. What do you like to do with your family?
16. If you could change the way you use your out-of-school time, what would you do?
17. What do you do each season? How would you change these things if you could?
18. What places around where you live would you like to go to more often?
19. What is your best time of day? Why?
20. What is your worst time of day? Why?
21. When have you been the happiest in your life? Describe it, think about it, talk about it.

CHART 2:

Yes, No, and Maybe

This chart is a list of activities that many children your age enjoy. Fill out the chart. You might enjoy putting stick-on dots beside the activities that you'd like to try. Also, for many children your age, the "Maybe I'd like to do this" category is helpful. Then think about the things you really like to do and find the contests that go along with those interests. This chart can also give you ideas for contests you might want to run for other kids.

1. Athletic Activities	YES, I'd like to do this	NO, I don't want to do this	MAYBE I'd like to do this
Aerobics			
Archery			
Badminton			
Baseball			
Basketball			
Baton twirling			
Bicycling			
Boating			
Bowling			
Canoeing			
Cross-country skiing			
Darts			
Downhill skiing			
Fencing			
Field hockey			
Fishing			
Football			
Frisbee			
Golf			

	YES, I'd like to do this	NO, I don't want to do this	MAYBE I'd like to do this
Gymnastics			
Hiking			
Horseback riding			
Horseshoes			
Ice hockey			
Ice-skating			
Jogging			
Judo			
Juggling			
Jumping rope			
Karate			
Kayaking			
Kite flying			
Paddle boating			
Paddle tennis			
Racquetball			
Rodeo			
Roller-blading			
Roller-skating			
Sailing			
Self-defense arts			
Skateboarding			
Soccer			
Softball			
Street hockey			
Surfing			
Swimming			
Tai Chi			
Tennis			
Track and field			
Water games			

	YES, I'd like to do this	NO, I don't want to do this	MAYBE I'd like to do this
Waterskiing			
Wrestling			
Yoga			
2. Cultural Activities			
ARTS AND CRAFTS			
Architectural design			
Batik			
Cake decorating			
Calligraphy			
Candle making			
Carpentry			
Cartoon drawing			
Ceramics			
Crochet			
Decoupage (collage)			
Designing and making posters			
Doll making and doll house making			
Doodle art			
Dough art			
Embroidery			
Fabric painting			
Free-hand drawing			
Illustrating stories			
Kite making			
Knitting			
Macrame			
Mathematical art			
Model building			
Mural painting			
Needlepoint			
Oil painting			

	YES, I'd like to do this	NO, I don't want to do this	MAYBE I'd like to do this
Origami			
Photography			
Pottery			
Printmaking			
Puppet making			
Quilting			
Rug making			
Sand sculpting			
Sculpting			
Sewing			
Tie-dyeing			
Watercolor			
Weaving			
Woodcraft and woodworking			
DANCE			
Ballet			
Ballroom dance			
Belly dance			
Creative movement			
Folk dance (i.e., African, Greek, Irish, Latin)			
Jazz dance			
Modern dance			
Square dance			
Swing dance			
Tap dance			
DRAMA			
Choral reading			
Clown lessons			
Community theatre			
Costuming			
Dramatization			

	YES, I'd like to do this	NO, I don't want to do this	MAYBE I'd like to do this
Face painting			
Improvisation			
Magic tricks and card tricks			
Makeup workshop			
Mask making			
Mime			
Play production			
Play writing			
Prop making			
Puppetry			
Role-playing			
Set construction			
Story telling			
Theatre games			
Ventriloquism			
MUSIC			
Band			
Chamber music			
Choir			
Chorus			
Composing music			
Making instruments			
Musical instrument lessons			
accordion			
autoharp			
cello			
clarinet			
cornet			
cymbals			
drums			
flute			
gong			

	YES, I'd like to do this	NO, I don't want to do this	MAYBE I'd like to do this
Musical instrument lessons *(cont'd)*			
guitar			
harmonica			
maracas			
oboe			
organ			
piano			
piccolo			
recorder			
saxophone			
tambourine			
triangle			
trombone			
trumpet			
viola			
violin			
xylophone			
Music appreciation			
Opera			
Rock 'n' roll			
Song writing			
Voice lessons			
3. Civic and Community Activities			
American National Red Cross Programs			
Art programs			
Big Brother/Big Sister Association			
Boys Clubs of America			
Boy Scouts of America			
Camp Fire, Inc.			
Collectors' clubs			
Community newspaper			
Computer clubs			

	YES, I'd like to do this	NO, I don't want to do this	MAYBE I'd like to do this
Educational groups (study of mammals, study of rocks)			
Ethnic activities			
Extended day and after-school programs			
4-H programs			
Friendship clubs			
Garden and horticultural groups			
Girls Clubs of America			
Girl Scouts of America			
Historical societies			
Hobby clubs			
Humane Society (taking care of animals)			
Jobs (clean, care for another person, care for a pet, get a paper route, sell baked goods and candy)			
Language clubs (French, Spanish, Italian, German)			
Library and reading clubs			
Nature clubs			
Pupil-to-pupil programs (send a notebook or other school supplies to a student in a developing country)			
Religious activities			
Special needs organizations (gifted, handicapped, etc.)			
Sports/fitness programs			
Student letter exchange (pen pals in another country)			
Town, recreation, community, and special programs			
Volunteer programs			
Writing clubs			
YMCA and YWCA			

4. Outdoor and Nature Activities

	YES, I'd like to do this	NO, I don't want to do this	MAYBE I'd like to do this
Animal farm or shelter—study the animals			
Archeological program—attend and participate in a dig			
Astronomy—view the constellations through a telescope			
Audubon sanctuary—take a guided walk or tour			
Audubon societies—join a youth program			
Backpacking—go on an extended adventure			
Beach—walking, building sand castles, and studying life			
Bird watching			
Botanical gardens—explore and study			
Build a birdfeeder—record the birds			
Butterflies—catch and classify			
Cranberry bog or blueberry farm—visit and study the process			
Forests—explore			
Geology—collect, identify, and polish rocks			
Historical sights and neighborhoods—take a walking tour			
Islands—visit one and study life on it			
Life on a river—study it			
Mountain climbing			
Natural history—join a club			
Nature centers—attend a local program			
Nature craft activities—use all natural materials			
Plant a garden—flower or vegetable			
Pond life—explore it			
Science—attend classes and workshops at museums and planetaria, solve problems			
Shell collecting			
Trees, shrubs, and flowers—study and classify			

	YES, I'd like to do this	NO, I don't want to do this	MAYBE I'd like to do this
Whale watching—go on an expedition and learn about whales			
Wild edible plants—study and classify			
Winter environment—explore			
Zoo—visit and study the animals			

5. Developing Special Interests

	YES, I'd like to do this	NO, I don't want to do this	MAYBE I'd like to do this
Animals—adopt and care for one			
Archeology—go on a dig			
Astrology—study the stars, moon, and sun and their influences on our lives			
Aviation—learn about planes			
Cars—learn about old and new models			
C.B. radio			
Chemistry—begin to experiment			
Collecting—baseball cards, coins, dolls (and doll clothes and houses), miniature cars, railroad cars and trains, stamps, etc.			
Computers—learn LOGOwriter or BASIC			
Cooking and nutrition			
Creating poems			
Crossword puzzles and word games			
Designing and writing—ad copy, greeting cards, logos			
Entomology—study insects and their habits			
Experimenting with electricity			
Film—make your own home movies			
Finance—set up your own bank account, keep track of your spending			
Game playing—backgammon, billiards, card games, checkers, chess, Clue, computer games, cribbage, designing code games, Dungeons and Dragons, Masterpiece, Monopoly, pool, simulation games, etc.			
Genealogy—study your family history, make a tree, write stories of your grandparents' childhoods			

	YES, I'd like to do this	NO, I don't want to do this	MAYBE I'd like to do this
Geography—buy a map of your state, buy a globe			
History—study a period you're interested in			
Humor—write jokes, tell riddles, and read and draw comics			
Journalism—write newspaper stories, ad copy, and press releases			
Languages—learn Spanish, French, Italian, Greek, German, etc.			
Learn about people from different countries			
Magic—practice tricks and perform shows			
Make a terrarium			
Make treats—candy with molds, ice cream, cookies, no-bake snacks			
Math games—solve math problems			
Meditation			
Mind-stretchers and mind games			
Model car and plane construction and racing			
Navigation—map out your next trip			
Outer space and UFOs			
Pets—training and grooming			
Pogo-sticking			
Puzzles—complete 500 or 1,000 pieces and frame			
Radio announcing, taping interviews, and doing productions			
Read books about famous people			
Read books of your choice and keep a record of them			
Research your town's activities			
Sign language			
Take a "transportation" ride just for fun— train, boat, plane			
Write a pen pal			
Write (books, newspapers, poems, plays, commercials, and folk tales)			

6. Places to Visit	YES, I'd like to visit this	NO, I don't want to visit this	MAYBE I'd like to visit this
Airport			
Aquarium			
Bakery			
Ballet recital			
Book publisher			
Brewery or bottling company			
Candle factory			
Car manufacturing plant			
Cereal factory			
Circus			
Clothing manufacturer			
Computer company or store			
Courthouse or state capitol			
Farmers' market			
Greenhouse			
Historical site			
Hotel			
Library			
Modeling school			
Movies			
Museums (art, science, children's, transportation)			
Music concert			
Newspaper publisher			
Parents' place of work			
Parks (bring a picnic)			
Planetarium			
Printing company			
Puppet show			
Radio or TV station			
Sports event			

	YES, I'd like to visit this	NO, I don't want to visit this	MAYBE I'd like to visit this
Sugar factory			
Telephone company			
Theatre			
Top of a tall building			
Toy manufacturer			

CHART 3:

Contest Finder

This chart will help you find a contest to enter any month of the year. Only those contests with specific dates have been listed here.

January:

American Association of Retired Persons (AARP) Intergenerational Program Awards (Girls Clubs), p. 226

Annual Speed Rope Jumping Contest, p. 100

Awards for Fundraising Activities (Girls Clubs), p. 228

Boys Clubs of America Young Artists Program—Fine Arts Exhibit Program, p. 204

Eastman Kodak Photography Contest (Girls Clubs), p. 216

Eastman Kodak Photography Program Grant Awards (Girls Clubs), p. 230

Girls Clubs of America Expansion Awards, p. 231

Girls Clubs of America Outstanding Program Awards, p. 233

McCall's Sewing Program Awards (Girls Clubs), p. 235

Morgan Horse Art Contest, p. 20

National Make It Yourself with Wool Competition, p. 41

Ocean Pals, p. 21

Publish-A-Book Contest, p. 191

State Times and Morning Advocate Current Events Rally, p. 182

February:

Boston Public Schools/Aardvark Systems and Programming, Inc. Elementary, Middle, and High School Computer Competition, p. 46

Boys Clubs of America Honor Awards for Program Excellence, p. 224

Boys Clubs of America Young Artists Program—Photography, p. 207

BMI Music Awards to Student Composers, p. 25

National Federation of Music Clubs Jr. Festivals—through April, p. 28

P. A. Witty Outstanding Literature Award, p. 80

World Championship Crab Races, p. 152

March:

April:

May:

June:

July:

The Activities Club®

The Activities Club® is an innovative new program that introduces school-age children to exciting hobbies and long-term interests. Every month, club members receive kits in the mail acquainting them with fascinating new subjects, such as photography, magic, astronomy, and bird watching. Each kit includes a terrific new project, club letter, activity cards, iron-on badge and more. Members also receive awards, certificates, and birthday greetings. Through the club letter, members participate in contests and share ideas with members across the country.

DESCRIPTIONS OF ACTIVITY KITS:

► **The Welcome to the Club Kit** contains an official club T-shirt, fabric markers, a poster and top-secret door hanger, and an official member iron-on theme badge. Everything comes in a storage box, which is perfect for keeping club stuff. The club letter has directions for children to set up their own clubs, while activity cards have tips on how to design secret club codes, make club snacks, and more. Everything needed to set up a club house or meeting area is included.

► **The Photography Kit** has a 35 mm camera, film, club letter, activity cards, iron-on camera badge, and a "Do Not Disturb" sign. The club letter is packed with information on picture taking and experimenting with photography. Activity cards describe how to mount and frame a photo and create a family "picture" tree.

► **The Magic Kit** has four magic tricks, a magic wand, a book of tricks, and an iron-on badge. The club letter focuses on the history of magic and the lives of famous magicians. Activity cards describe how to perform lots of coin and card tricks and how to make props for magic shows.

► **The Safari Rubber Stamps Kit** features a set of six wild animal stamps, ink pad, glitter glue, and giraffe iron-on badge. There is also a frame for master creations. Activity cards explain how to make stationery and wrapping paper, create comic strips, enter postcard contests, and more. The club letter offers additional stamping projects.

► **The Bird Kit** has a wooden bird feeder, bird chart, iron-on bird badge, and bird seed. The club letter has tips on bird watching, and activity cards contain directions for making bird mobiles and bird baths. There are also directions for over 15 other easy-to-make bird feeders.

► **The Mask Kit** has materials to make African and cat masks, and also contains a mask iron-on badge. The club letter and activity cards offer directions for a variety of additional masks including papier mâché and theater masks.

▶ **The Universe Kit** features a glow-in-the-dark Map of the Universe and Glow Stars as well as a star iron-on badge. The club letter has information about stars and constellations and an interview with a space shuttle astronaut. Activity cards offer suggestions for additional activities and a contest.

▶ **The Sea Life Kit** features a wooden shark model, miniature squid, Undersea World Rummy cards, and sea life iron-on badge. The club letter is packed with information about sea life and The Cousteau Society, and activity cards contain additional projects, such as a sailor's valentine and a sea mobile.

▶ **The Cooking Kit** has an ice cream maker, chef's apron, materials to make chef's hats, measuring set, and cooking tools. An iron-on badge is also included. The club letter has tips for planning and cooking healthy menus. Activity cards are full of great recipes for drinks, crunchy snacks, ice cream and frozen treats, salads, and fun meals.

▶ **The Gift Kit** contains materials to make creative gifts for grandparents, parents, relatives, teachers, and friends. It includes Pour and Paint® molds for decorative magnets, ornaments, pins and pendants, as well as fabric and patterns for making puppets. It also features a club letter, iron-on badge, and activity cards full of additional gift-making projects.

▶ **The Games Kit** features terrific games to play indoors and out including Shut the Box, Bubble Fingers, marbles, and a tangram. The club letter tells about the history of games, how to make a rainy day game box, and much more. Activity cards have games from around the world and tell how to make up your own games. There is also an iron-on badge.

▶ **Kit Twelve: A Surprise!** The key word in the club is "active." Active members enjoy fun-filled indoor and outdoor activities with each kit. The club stamps out boredom during afternoons, evenings, weekends, and vacations!

Dear Parent,

"I'm bored. I'm bored. I'm bored." Every child, even the most active, has said it, and every parent has heard it and wondered what to do.

What You As a Parent Can Do...

Helping your child discover natural abilities and then reinforcing those abilities is what we all strive to do as parents. But the main goal is to have *fun* doing it!

The Activities Club helps your child to develop lifelong hobbies and to explore new interests. Club members receive activity kits in the mail, such as Photography, Magic, The Universe, Birds, Mask Making, Cooking, Sea Life, Making Gifts, Games, and more. Each kit includes an exciting project, a club letter full of information, activity cards with games and contests, an iron-on badge, and lots of surprises.

The Activities Club was created to make your job easier and more rewarding. The club provides fascinating projects and activities designed to appeal to your child's senses of curiosity, exploration, and, most of all, fun!

For Kids Only...

The Activities Club is for children ages 6 to 12. It is *their* club. Every aspect of the club has been designed to recognize and reward their involvement and initiative. Each member has opportunities to enter contests, send away for freebies, have their work published, contribute activity ideas, get mail back from the club, and much, much more. It's truly interactive!

Of the kids, by the kids, and for the kids, The Activities Club helps children develop a sense of belonging, but also equally important senses of self-direction and self-esteem.

Here's How It Works...

Sign up for The Activities Club now, and your child will start to receive Activities Club Kits monthly in the mail. Choose a series of six or twelve kits or try them individually. Kids love getting their own mail, so the fun begins the minute each package arrives.

Please take a moment to look at the description of kits on the previous pages. Then return the order form on the following page or call to order.

Enroll your child in The Activities Club today. Let your child discover a whole new world of interests right in your home.

Sincerely,

Joan Bergstrom
President

P.S. FREE BONUS—When you pay for a series of twelve kits, we'll send your child a special birthday kit.

P.P.S. Call 1-800-873-5487 now to enroll your child today!

MEMBERSHIP FORM

Child's name _____

Birthday _____

Street _____

City/State/Zip _____

Phone number _____

❑ I have enclosed $12.95 plus $2.95 shipping and handling for The Welcome to the Club Kit. Shipments to MA add $.65 tax. (Savings of $1.) I understand my child will receive kits monthly unless I choose to cancel our membership.

❑ I have enclosed payment of $180, which includes shipping and handling for a series of 12 Activity Kits. Shipments to MA add $7.23 tax. (Savings of $22.80.) Kits will be mailed monthly.

FREE BONUS (with orders of 12 kits): A special Birthday Kit is sent to your child as a present.

❑ I have enclosed payment of $92.70, which includes shipping and handling for a series of 6 Activity Kits. Shipments to MA add $3.75 tax. (Savings of $8.70.) Kits will be mailed monthly for 6 months.

❑ Please send me the most current information on The Activities Club®.

❑ CHECK ENCLOSED   ❑ MASTERCARD   ❑ VISA

CARD NUMBER _____

EXPIRATION DATE _____

Adult's name _____

Street _____

City/State/Zip _____

Phone number _____

THE ACTIVITIES CLUB®
P.O. BOX 9104 • WALTHAM, MASSACHUSETTS 02254-9104

1-800-873-5487   CALL FOR FASTER SERVICE!

About the Authors

Joan M. Bergstrom, Ed.D. is the author of the widely acclaimed book *School's Out* (published in 1984 and revised in 1990). Dr. Bergstrom is president of The Activities Club® in Waltham, Massachusetts, where she is involved in designing creative, fun, and innovative activity kits. The Activities Club® is a program in which children six to twelve receive fascinating projects and activities designed to stimulate their curiosity. Children explore hobbies in fun and creative ways in their out-of-school time. Dr. Bergstrom is also a professor in the graduate and undergraduate divisions at Wheelock College in Boston, Massachusetts. Over the past ten years, Dr. Bergstrom has written on children's use of out-of-school time for publications such as *Good Housekeeping, Working Mother, McCall's, Better Homes and Gardens, PTA Today, Instructor, The New York Daily News, USA Today, The Christian Science Monitor,* and others. She has appeared on more than 60 television and radio shows in the United States, Australia, and Singapore discussing this topic.

Craig G. Bergstrom has conducted many workshops on out-of-school activities and safety for school-age children. He has also done a number of television and radio shows on these subjects. Bergstrom graduated from the Belmont Hill School in Belmont, Massachusetts, and currently attends Dartmouth College.

Our thanks to the authors of "words of wisdom" appearing throughout ALL THE BEST CONTESTS FOR KIDS.

Michael Andersen, Lelhia Baker, Britany Bauer, Pauline Baughman, Brandon Bauman, Debby Bestul, Carol Blanchet-Ruth, Elizabeth Brown, Jasmin Burgas, Laura Butera, Paul Calandrella, Karah Card, Brian Carlson, Gene Chan, Kalonda Chance, Kristin Chevalier, Cammy Clark, Marie Condron, Gary Costanzo, Melissa Cox, Matt Crecelius, Joy Croft, Dannette Cruse, Emily Davidson, Sherry Deckman, Jamie Dewitt, Kelly Dona, Lisa Dore, Theresa Dovan, Noah Duarte, Stanley Ehrhardt, Sarah Eckert, Rachel Evans, Rachael Facciolla, Kirk Faulstich, Richard Ferrara, Tricia Finnegan, Kristy Fischer, Alan Francis, Corinne Frederick, Karen Galvin, Kathy Garruba, Amy Hagstrom, Tamir Halaban, Natalie Hoepp, Peter Honig, Brande Nicole Hudelson, Mary Illingworth, Ted Iszler, John Jackman, Leslie Jones, Will Klopenstein, Perry Korzenowski, Tonya Kouri, Allison Kuklok, Krista Kunze, Lisa Ann Labadie, Robbie Lanning, Lisa Lashley, Brian La Voie, Michelle Link, Brian Lloyd, Lucas Lorenz, Josephine Marrero, Emily Martin, Brandon Mason, Kevin McCabe, Devon McClain, Sandy McLachlin, Mike Mielnicki, Alicia Miller, Rex Min, Cadie Morning, Corey Morning, Jennifer Mosher, Eamonn Murry, Balu Natarajan, Alicia Neil, Michelle Nigalan, Kellie O'Shields, Jon Pennington, Heather Peppard, Andrea Pinkus, David Prosser, Tobey Reynolds, Bo Roberts, Stephanie Roberts, Teri Rorabaugh, Jonathan Rosenbaum, Nicholas Saeger, Brett Samber, Kristofer Savial, John Schade, Denise Schulze, Daree Serrano, Abby Shoemaker, Kathy Skilaris, Nikisha Small, Michael Spors, Elizabeth Stallone, Chad Steinmetz, Karen Stewart, Jenni Strunk, Tami Jo Sullivan, Mike Taylor, Tucker Thompson, Benjamin Turek, Nicole Tygielski, Jackie Walker, Graham Watson, Lynn Wegescheide, Cathy West, Lee Whaley, Isaac Whitlatch, and Leanne Yamada.